JERRY THOME

French Alps Travel Guide 2023, 2024 and Beyond

Your Companion to France's Mountain Paradise

Contents

Preface

Close your eyes and see beautiful lakes reflecting the sparkling sunlight, a symphony of alpine flowers swaying in the mild breeze, and majestic snow-capped peaks stretching as far as the eye can see. The French Alps are an unparalleled experience and a genuine work of art in the natural world.

The French Alps are, above all, an outdoor lover's dream come true. You'll find everything you're looking for here, whether you're an adrenaline addict in search of exhilarating experiences or a nature lover desiring peace and quiet. With well-known ski resorts like Chamonix-Mont-Blanc luring you to sculpt your way down snowy slopes, the area is a haven for skiers and snowboarders. Can you picture the thrill of gliding across powder-soft snow while taking in breathtaking views of the mountains?

But the Alps provide more than just winter wonderland splendor; the summer months open up a whole other realm of discovery. There are plenty of options for hiking and trekking, which take you up difficult mountain slopes and into lush valleys. With each step you take, the breathtaking scenery will enthrall you and captivate your senses.

Speaking of beauty, the towns and villages tucked away in the French Alps are like something from a storybook. Known as the "Venice of the Alps," Annecy is a gorgeous jewel with its cobblestone streets lined with colorful buildings and quaint waterways. Its rustic appeal will enchant you as you take in the pleasant ambiance. Another must-see location that combines urban energy with alpine allure is Grenoble, a bustling university city encircled by mountains.

Let's now discuss the regional food, which will take your taste buds on a lovely voyage. Some of the most delicious foods you'll ever taste may be found in the French Alps. Every bite will be a culinary revelation, from the well-known fondue and raclette, where warm, crusty bread and melted cheese meet, to the savory tartiflette and robust raclette potatoes. These delicacies make for a divine feast suitable for a king or queen when paired with fine wines from the area.

But the rich cultural tapestry woven throughout the area will enchant you more than the cuisine alone. The French Alps are home to a plethora of customs and celebrations that unite local communities. See for yourself how kind the people are as they freely share their traditions and tales. Immerse yourself in the vibrant festivals that will create lasting memories in your soul. These events fill the mountain air with music, dancing, and laughing.

Traveling through the French Alps will also take you to a place where you may heal and regenerate. Accept the therapeutic benefits of thermal spas, where mineral-rich waters gushing from centuries-old springs can calm your body and spirit. Give yourself permission to relax in the peaceful surroundings and come home with a whole new lease on life.

Additionally, you can travel through the area sustainably to make sure that your trip has a beneficial effect on the local economy and ecology. By following responsible tourism practices, you may contribute to the French Alps' conservation efforts to maintain their natural beauty.

There you have it, my friend—a sneak peek at the seductive charm of the French Alps. Insightful experiences, stunning scenery, delectable food, and cultural immersion are all available in the French Alps, making it an unforgettable trip. Get ready to fall deeply in love with this winter wonderland and make lifelong memories that will bring you joy. The trip of a lifetime starts here as the French Alps welcome you.

I

Welcome to the French Alps!

1

The Geography

In southeast France, the French Alps, also known as the "Alpes françaises" in French, are a stunning mountain range that shares borders with Switzerland and Italy. These magnificent mountains form an amazing backdrop of towering peaks and verdant valleys, spanning over 750 miles (1,200 kilometers) across the nation.

The highest peak in Western Europe, the Mont Blanc massif, is located in the center of the French Alps and rises to a height of 4,810 meters (15,781 feet) above sea level. With its majestic appearance and snow-capped summit, this well-known mountain commands attention from onlookers and commands the entire environment.

Mont Blanc

There are multiple separate regions within the Alps, each with its distinct topography and character. The northernmost regions include the Chablais and the Bornes Massif, which are renowned for their verdant landscapes, profound lakes, and quaint alpine communities. The Aravis Range, with its craggy limestone peaks that draw rock climbers from all over the world, will come into view as you proceed south.

As you proceed south, you'll come to the Tarentaise Valley, which is home to some of the most well-known ski areas worldwide. With world-class winter sports facilities available in towns like Val d'Isère, Tignes, and Courchevel, the wide, open valleys here are ideal for skiing and snowboarding.

The Maurienne Valley, which connects France with Italy across the Alps, is located to the east and is well-known for its historical significance. Road bikers will find bliss in this region because of its twisting roads, steep slopes, and quaint villages.

Hikers and mountaineers will find refuge in the Ecrins National Park as you continue your journey across the French Alps. This protected region is the perfect place for nature enthusiasts looking for peace and quiet because it has glaciers, alpine meadows, and a variety of species.

The Vanoise National Park, France's first national park, is a must-see destination situated amidst the Graian Alps. Numerous endangered species find refuge in the park, which offers a glimpse of the pristine grandeur of the Alps through its beautiful valleys and towering peaks.

As you continue south, you'll reach the Dauphiné Alps, which are ideal for trekking and climbing excursions due to their combination of towering peaks and deep valleys. Remember to take a look at the charming towns scattered around this area; each has a unique rich cultural history and traditions.

The French Alps' topography includes more than simply mountains and valleys; tranquil glacier lakes also contribute to the area's allure. For instance, Lake Annecy is well-known for both its glistening pure waters and the breathtaking mountain scenery that surrounds it.

In addition to their stunning natural surroundings, the French Alps are home to numerous little alpine towns that continue to practice their ancient customs. Every community has something interesting to say, from unique architecture to delectable regional cuisine.

2

Effective Planning

When to Visit

The French Alps are a year-round destination that has something special to offer in every season thanks to their breathtaking scenery and wide variety of activities. The ideal time to visit this wonderland of the mountains will mostly rely on your tastes, interests, and desired experience.

The French Alps are stunning throughout the winter when the area is transformed into a pure snowy wonderland. Skiers and snowboarders eager to conquer world-class ski resorts like Chamonix-Mont-Blanc, Courchevel, and Val d'Isère fill the slopes from December to February. This is the perfect time to go to the slopes if you love winter sports and want to feel the rush of floating down powdery terrain.

In addition to skiing and snowboarding, wintertime offers a wide range of other enjoyable activities. Try your hand at dog sledding, go on thrilling snowshoeing excursions, or just take in the tranquil beauty of the snow-covered countryside. Enjoy warm fondues, cozy up in quaint chalets, and take in the wonder of the Christmas markets, which bring cheer and a festive atmosphere to the air.

The French Alps are awakened by spring with a rush of color and activity as winter gradually bids adieu. From March to May, the alpine landscape is transformed from snowy landscapes into vivid greens, with blossoming flowers and sprouting trees creating a stunning tapestry. Hiking aficionados will find that the spring offers beautiful views and pleasant temperatures on the routes that open up.

Enjoy the peaceful serenity before the summer throngs arrive, and see the valleys come alive with wildflowers. Opportunities for further outdoor pursuits like paragliding and mountain biking also arise in the spring. It's a season of rebirth for the natural world as well as for tourists looking for a more serene and reflective experience among the Alps' natural treasures.

In the French Alps, summer is peak season, and for good reason. The area comes alive with a wide variety of activities for any traveler's taste from June to August. There are many other outdoor activities available throughout the warmer months, such as white-water rafting, canyoning, and rock climbing. Enjoy the longer daylight hours by going on as much exploration as you choose.

The opportunity to travel to high-altitude regions that were closed off by snow throughout the winter is one of the best things about summer. Experience amazing views, undiscovered alpine lakes, and magnificent mountain passes. A vibrant cultural calendar is also brought about by summer when regional celebrations of customs that have been passed down through the ages take place.

Autumn casts a warm, golden hue over the French Alps as summer ends. A more sedate and reflective experience can be had from September through November. As the leaves change color, nature puts on a breathtaking show of vivid colors, and the crowds thin out.

For those who want to experience peace and beautiful scenery without the hustle and bustle of summer, autumn is the perfect season. The hiking paths are still open, providing a chance to enjoy the clean mountain air and breathtaking fall foliage. Harvest festivities take place during this time, and it's an opportunity to savor the region's seasonal specialties, such as freshly gathered chestnuts and mushrooms.

Packing Essentials

To get the most out of your trip and enjoy the amazing scenery and experiences that the Alps have to offer, you must prepare wisely. Please remember the following crucial points:

1. Remember to pack any document you'll need for your trip! This covers your passport, travel insurance, identification, and any permissions needed for particular Alps activities or regions.

2. Since the weather in the Alps can change drastically, bring items that are appropriate for any season. On warm days, pack

8

airy and light clothing, such as shorts and t-shirts. However, don't forget to bring along some additional warm layers, such as jackets, sweaters, and even a water-resistant raincoat. Thermal clothing is also a smart addition for chilly days and nights.

2. If you intend to hike or explore the mountain paths, you should wear strong, comfortable footwear. Don't forget to bring along a pair of supportive hiking boots that fit nicely around the ankle. You can wear comfortable sneakers or walking shoes for casual occasions.

3. Outdoor activities might result in small cuts and scrapes. Stow adhesive bandages, antiseptic wipes, painkillers, and other personal drugs you might require in a tiny first-aid kit.

4. Because the sun may be very strong in the highlands, bring sun protection items like broad-brimmed hats or caps, sunglasses, and high-SPF sunscreen. It's important to wear protective gear for your skin and eyes when enjoying the Alpine outdoors.

5. For your travels, a well-made backpack will be your greatest friend. It ought to have adequate room for your necessities, including a map, a camera, water bottles, food, and a first aid kit. For shorter trips, a smaller daypack may be useful.

6. It's important to stay hydrated, particularly at higher elevations. If you always have a reusable water bottle with you, you may simply fill it up from the mountains' natural springs and streams.

7. To keep your electronics charged when traveling, don't forget to pack a universal travel adaptor. Additionally useful is a power bank, particularly if you intend to spend a lot of time outside.

8. The French Alps provide breathtaking sweeping vistas and the chance to see wildlife. Thus, remember to pack binoculars and a camera or smartphone with a good camera so you may record those priceless moments.

10. A Swiss Army Knife or Multi-tool is a multipurpose tool that can come in helpful for a variety of tasks, such as doing tiny repairs on your equipment or chopping fruits during a picnic.

11. Bring a Lightweight Towel: Whether you're taking a cool plunge in a mountain lake or need to wipe off some perspiration while hiking, a little, fast-drying towel comes in handy.

12. Bringing along some foldable and reusable bags will be helpful, particularly if you intend to shop or want to bring some locally produced goods home.

Though packing is necessary, try to pack as little as possible. Pay attention to the essentials and things that will improve your time in the French Alps.

3

Entering the Alps

The trip to the French Alps is one of excitement and expectation. Travelers from all over the world can reach this breathtaking alpine area because of the multitude of transportation choices available. There are numerous ways to start your alpine experience, including inexpensive international flights, well-functioning train systems, and breathtaking road excursions. Together, we can investigate the different ways to get to the French Alps and ensure that your trip is as effortless as newly groomed ski slopes.

1. **By Air**: Several significant airports that service the area serve as the main international entry point to the French Alps. Here are a few important airports to think about:

- **Geneva International Airport (GVA):** This airport serves as a major entrance point for visitors to the northern French Alps and is located on the border between France and Switzerland. It provides a handy entry point to well-known ski resorts like Chamonix, Morzine, and Avoriaz and serves important international airlines. You have three options for getting to your destination from Geneva: shared shuttle services, private transfers, or auto rentals.

- **Lyon-Saint Exupéry Airport (LYS):** This airport, which is close to Lyon, offers access to the French Alps on the north and south. Traveling to well-known locations like Grenoble, Annecy, and Chambéry is simple from here. The airport is served by major airlines and has good connections to several locations in Europe.

- **Chambéry Airport (CMF):** This airport serves as the gateway to some French Alps ski destinations, including Val d'Isère, Méribel, and Courchevel. It receives a lot of seasonal flights in the winter, which makes it a good choice for those looking for easy access to the slopes.

- **Grenoble-Alpes-Isère Airport (GNB):** This airport is conveniently located close to Grenoble and provides a great entry point to the Southern French Alps. With flights from several European cities, it's especially well-liked by skiers going to adjacent resorts like Les Deux Alpes and Alpe d'Huez.

- **Nice Côte d'Azur Airport (NCE):** Although it is farther from the major Alpine region, Nice Airport is a good choice for tourists who want to combine an experience in the mountains with a vacation to the French Riviera. To get to locations in the Southern Alps, you can rent a car or take the train from Nice.

2. **By Train:** Train travel is a desirable way to see the French Alps because France has a vast and well-functioning railway network. High-speed trains (TGV) run by the French National

Railway Company (SNCF) link major towns with destinations in the Alps. These are a few important train lines:

- Paris to Lyon: Lyon is a significant transportation center in the region and can be reached by TGV train from Paris. You can change to regional trains from Lyon to get to several cities and villages in the Alps.

- Paris to Chambéry or Grenoble: Taking a TGV train from Paris to Chambéry or Grenoble is an additional option that provides quick access to the Northern and Southern French Alps, respectively.

- Geneva to Chamonix: The Mont-Blanc Express is a charming train trip that departs from Geneva and arrives in Chamonix, offering breathtaking Alps vistas all along the way.

- Milan to Chamonix: The Mont Blanc Express is a rail service that takes visitors from Italy from Milan to Chamonix.

- Eurostar Ski Train (London to the French Alps): In the winter, the Eurostar Ski Train runs direct routes from London to well-known ski resorts in the French Alps, including Bourg-Saint-Maurice, Moûtiers, and Aime-la-Plagne.

3. **By Car:** Traveling to the French Alps by car is a great way for people who value freedom and flexibility to take beautiful road adventures. Major cities and highways in France and its neighboring nations are well-connected to the Alps. The following are some estimated travel times from major cities:

From Geneva to Chamonix, it takes roughly one hour and fifteen minutes.

From Lyon to Chambéry: around one hour.

From Milan to Chamonix: Takes about three hours.

- Travel time from Paris to Grenoble: about 5 hours.

From Nice to Alpe d'Huez: Takes about four hours and thirty minutes.

Please be aware that certain mountain roads may experience snow and icy conditions during the winter, necessitating the use of snow chains or winter tires when driving.

4. **By Bus and Shuttle Services**: Some bus and shuttle services connect major train and airport hubs with a range of French Alps ski destinations. These services provide an affordable and practical means of getting to your destination.

5. **By Helicopter**: Helicopter transports from major airports to certain upscale ski resorts in the French Alps are offered for individuals looking for an opulent and quick trip. This option offers a breathtaking aerial experience that showcases the breathtaking mountain vistas from above.

4

Entry Requirements

Travelers from outside should take into account the French Alps' and France's overall visa and admission requirements before starting their alpine journey. Gaining insight into the visa policies and entry prerequisites guarantees a hassle-free and easy trip to this fascinating location. To help you confidently plan your trip to the French Alps, we'll go over the necessary travel documents, Schengen Area, visa-exempt countries, travel insurance, and visa rules here.

The Schengen Area, which consists of 26 European nations that have done away with passport controls at their shared borders and have a unified visa policy, includes France. This implies that, for a predetermined period, you are free to travel within the entire Schengen Area after you have obtained a visa for one of the member states. Since the French Alps are in France, they are covered by the Schengen visa regulations.

Certain nationals, including those of France, are not required to have a visa to enter the Schengen Area for brief visits. For up to 90 days during 180 days, citizens of these nations are not required to get a visa to enter the Schengen Area for travel, business, or family visits. The United States, Canada, the United Kingdom, Australia, New Zealand, Japan, and numerous EU members are among the nations that do not require a visa.

Before visiting the French Alps, if you are a citizen of a nation that is not on the list of nations exempt from requiring a visa, you must apply for a Schengen visa at the French embassy or consulate in your home country. Typically, the following paperwork is required for the visa application process:

- A current passport that has at least two blank pages and is valid for at least three months after the date you want to leave the Schengen Area.
- Passport-sized photos taken recently that adhere to certain standards.
- Filled out application for a visa.
- Evidence of lodging in the French Alps, such as a letter of invitation from a host or hotel reservations.
- Travel insurance with a minimum coverage of 30,000 euros that covers medical costs and repatriation for the length of your stay in the Schengen Area.
- Evidence of trip plans, such as an itinerary or airline tickets.
- Proof that you will have enough cash on hand to pay for all of your expenses while visiting.
- A cover letter explaining your travel schedule and motivation for visiting France.

You must apply for a visa well in advance of the dates you intend to travel, as processing time frames and fees can differ. Make sure you familiarize yourself with the particular protocols and requirements of the French consulate or embassy in your nation.

You might need to apply for a residency permit or a long-stay visa if you intend to stay in the French Alps for longer than ninety days. Visas for extended stays are appropriate for activities including employment, education, and family reunions. Long-stay visa applications are more complicated and may call for extra paperwork, such as an employment contract or an acceptance letter from a French university.

Please be aware of the following:

All visitors entering the Schengen Area must have valid travel insurance. It needs to cover repatriation, medical emergencies, and other unanticipated events for the whole time you are visiting. Make sure your travel insurance covers at least 30,000 euros, the minimum amount required by the Schengen Area.

You might be required to present documentation of your accommodations in the French Alps, such as hotel reservations or a host's invitation letter while requesting a visa or entering the Schengen Area. You should also be able to prove that you have enough money to pay for all of your costs while you're there.

Carefully check your visa's validity and conditions before heading to the French Alps. If you want to visit nearby Schengen countries while on your trip, make sure your visa permits multiple entries. If you overstay your visa's validity, you may be subject to fines, have your visa revoked, or have trouble getting another one in the future.

You must ask for an extension through the French prefecture or town hall in your area if you want to stay longer in the French Alps than the amount of time allowed by your visa. Keep in mind that requests for visa extensions are subject to certain requirements and are not guaranteed.

The procedures for obtaining a visa may vary for passengers under particular conditions, such as those holding official or diplomatic passports, nationals of certain nations with bilateral agreements, or refugees. To find out the exact steps and conditions that apply to your case, contact the French embassy or consulate that is closest to you.

II

Explore The Regions of the French Alps

5

Haute-Savoie

Nestled in the southeast of France, Haute-Savoie is a melting pot of varied influences, bordering both Switzerland and Italy. The area is well-known for its striking valleys, glittering lakes, and snow-capped mountains. The tall peaks of Mont Blanc, the highest peak in Western Europe, which dominates the skyline and acts as a focal point for outdoor lovers and mountaineers, welcome you as you enter this alluring country. Come with me as we explore this amazing region within the French Alps!

Annecy

Situated in the Haute-Savoie area of France, this little town is yet another incredible find. All who visit Annecy are enthralled, with the city's fairytale-like beauty, breathtaking scenery, and extensive history making a lasting impression on their spirits.

Located near the shores of Lake Annecy, which is frequently referred to be the cleanest lake in Europe, this charming town offers a delightful fusion of the natural world and cultural legacy.

The lake's crystal-clear waters mirror the surrounding mountains, creating a stunning scene that changes with the seasons.

The "Vieille Ville," or ancient town of Annecy, is a picture-perfect location. You can feel as though you've traveled back in time as you stroll along its cobblestone alleys and take in the town's quaint canals and well-preserved medieval architecture. One of Annecy's most recognizable sites is the Palais de l'Isle, a castle from the 12th century that sits atop a little island in the Thiou River. It is now home to a local history museum after having been a prison in the past.

Strolling around the vibrant markets of Annecy is one of the most enjoyable activities there is. Tuesdays, Fridays, and Sundays see the Old Town Market, which is a veritable gold mine of regional cheeses, meats, fruits, and handcrafted goods. The market's vibrant ambiance and alluring aromas will tempt you to sample some of the mouthwatering cuisine from the area.

Lake Annecy is the focal point of the town's natural beauty, renowned for its pristine blue waters. Numerous water-based sports, including swimming, kayaking, paddleboarding, and even relaxing boat rides, are popular among both locals and tourists. The bicycle trail known as the "Tour du Lac," which circles the lake, is a lovely opportunity to explore the scenic shoreline and take in the breathtaking vistas at every bend.

If you have a passion for history, Annecy will not let you down. The Museum of Annecy is located in the Château d'Annecy, a magnificent medieval castle with a view of the town. Numerous historical relics, artistic creations, and enlightening glimpses into the town's past are on display at the museum.

The Museum

Annecy is a center of culture and the arts as well. Every year in June, animators, directors, and fans of animation from all over the world come to the International Animated Film Festival. The festival adds an artistic touch to the town's already lively atmosphere, celebrating the art of animation through screenings, workshops, and exhibitions.

Annecy comes alive in the sunny summer months with a plethora of festivals and events that highlight its joie de vivre. Thousands of people attend the Fête du Lac, a magnificent fireworks show above Lake Annecy, to see the vibrant pyrotechnics light up the night sky.

There are many options for outdoor sports in the landscape that surrounds the town. Hikers can explore the neighboring Semnoz Mountain, which provides sweeping views of the surrounding peaks and the entire Annecy region. Another amazing natural feature that is well worth seeing is the Gorges du Fier, a striking gorge sculpted by the Fier River.

Chamonix-Mont-Blanc

Located in the Haute-Savoie department of France, Chamonix-Mont-Blanc, or just Chamonix, is a magnificent mountain town that enthralls tourists with its imposing mountains, endearing atmosphere, and extensive history.

Standing at an astonishing 4,810 meters (15,781 feet) above sea level, the renowned Mont Blanc is the highest peak in Western Europe and the focal point of Chamonix-Mont-Blanc. Because the first successful climb of Mont Blanc occurred in Chamonix in 1786, the town's history is inextricably linked to mountaineering. Because of this historic achievement, Chamonix became known as a safe sanctuary for explorers and mountaineers from all over the world.

In Chamonix, winter is a magical season when the town is transformed into a wintry wonderland. A fresh coating of snow covers the neighboring mountains, enticing skiers and snowboarders to tackle the slopes. Chamonix provides winter sports fans with an exceptional experience, offering a variety of ski locations that appeal to all ability levels, from novices to expert powder hunters.

A trip on the Aiguille du Midi cable car is a must for any traveler to Chamonix. A breathtaking cable car trip will take you to the Aiguille du Midi peak, where you can enjoy breathtaking views of the surrounding valleys and the Mont Blanc massif. You will go on an exhilarating adventure into the high alpine realm, where you will be able to see some of the most breathtaking views in the entire region.

Summertime in Chamonix never gets old because of its breath-taking scenery and outdoor pursuits. With alpine vegetation and grassy meadows replacing snow-capped peaks, hiking and mountaineering become the main activities. Hikers from all over the world flock to the famed multi-day Tour du Mont Blanc, which circuits the Mont Blanc peak. It's an exciting and demanding trip that offers a close-up look at the breathtaking scenery of the area.

Chamonix has a lot of exciting things to offer to anyone who is looking for a rush, like rock climbing, white-water rafting, and paragliding. For those looking for an adrenaline rush and an opportunity to get in touch with nature differently, the surrounding mountains and deep gorges make the ideal playground.

In addition to being a destination for adventure, Chamonix-Mont-Blanc is a quaint town full of personality. The town center's pedestrianized lanes are dotted with quaint shops, cafés, and eateries offering mouthwatering Savoyard fare. After a day of outdoor activities, make sure to indulge in traditional meals like fondue, raclette, and tartiflette, which will warm your body and spirit.

Apart from its breathtaking scenery and outdoor activities, Chamonix has a thriving arts and culture scene. The town celebrates mountain culture, music, and the arts all year long with a variety of festivals and events. The Musée Alpin, a local alpine museum, displays early pioneers' gear and provides insight into the history of mountaineering in the area.

Additionally, both locals and visitors to Chamonix share a strong sense of community and friendship. The town exudes a sense of unity due to the friendly environment and common love of the mountains.

See the neighboring villages dispersed throughout the Chamonix Valley for a more serene experience. Charming alpine hamlets like Les Houches, Argentière, and Vallorcine offer a more tranquil respite from the busy urban center and a window into traditional mountain life.

Evian-les-Bains

Luxurious, restful, and rejuvenating are some of the feelings that come to mind when thinking of Evian-les-Bains, the graceful gem of the French Alps. Located in the Haute-Savoie area of France, this charming town is tucked away on the southern beaches of Lake Geneva. It has been known for its natural mineral water and thermal spas for generations. Evian-les-Bains is a popular destination for travelers from all over the world because of its luxurious Belle Époque architecture and immaculate lakefront.

The town's mineral water springs, which were found in the early 1800s, have a significant historical significance. The aristocracy and affluent began to frequent Evian as a spa destination after the mineral water from the Cachat Spring was discovered to have therapeutic qualities. The old pump room, reminiscent of the glitzy era of the town, is still open to visitors at the Cachat Spring. Savoring the mineral water that has made Evian-les-Bains renowned is one of the things that visitors must do there. The immaculate spring waters of the town provide the source of the Evian brand, which is well-known worldwide for its crisp flavor and purity. Wander around the public park known as the Jardins de l'Eau du Pré Curieux for a fun and instructive experience learning about the history of Evian's mineral water and the water cycle. Let's pause and learn something about this park:

Spanning over four hectares, these exquisitely designed gardens pay homage to the intrinsic beauty of water. Visitors engage in a sensory adventure as they stroll through a vast assortment of aquatic landscapes, from calm ponds filled with water lilies to babbling brooks and cascading waterfalls that induce a sense of tranquility and introspection.

What sets Jardins de l'Eau du Pré distinct is its blending of natural elements with artistic aspects. The garden serves as a canvas for sculptures, installations, and artistic compositions, effortlessly incorporated into the rich vegetation and water features. These artistic flourishes provide an extra dimension of beauty, enabling visitors to explore the interplay between art and nature in a calm atmosphere.

The garden's design is as useful as it is beautiful, exhibiting novel ways for water management and ecological balance. It's a living testament to sustainable landscaping principles, promoting a better understanding of environmental protection and responsible care of natural resources.

Visitors can engage in guided tours or walk at their speed, savoring the tranquil mood and capturing the gorgeous views that give moments of introspection and inspiration. Additionally, the garden conducts events, workshops, and educational activities, improving the visitor experience and promoting a deeper connection to the natural world.

With breathtaking views of Lake Geneva as its backdrop, Evian-les-Bains has a lot to offer when it comes to water sports. Visitors can enjoy swimming, sailing, and paddleboarding in the lake's crystal-clear waters, which let them appreciate this natural wonder's serene beauty. Savor the scenery of the lake's charming villages and surrounding mountains by taking a leisurely boat ride.

Evian-les-Bains is a paradise of opulent thermal spas and wellness facilities for visitors looking to unwind and rejuvenate. Offering a variety of decadent treatments, thermal pools, and expansive views of Lake Geneva, the Evian Spa at the Hôtel Royal is a haven of tranquility. Experience the restorative effects of the town's thermal baths, where you can relax in the centuries-old healing waters.

In addition, Evian-les-Bains is well known for its magnificent Belle Époque architecture, which elevates the town's atmosphere. Admire the imposing hotels and sumptuous homes that harken back to a bygone age as you stroll through the quaint alleyways. This architectural style is exemplified by the Palais Lumière, a former thermal spa that is now a cultural center that hosts art exhibitions and other activities.

There are many festivals and events held throughout the year, resulting in a lively and varied cultural environment in the town. Internationally recognized Evian Musical Encounters is a music event that draws celebrities and music enthusiasts to enjoy captivating shows in different locations throughout the city.

The Château de Ripaille is a must-visit location for history buffs. Not far from Evian-les-Bains, this medieval castle boasts lovely gardens and conducts guided trips that explore the area's rich past. This stately house, surrounded by lush forests and overlooking the peaceful waters of Lake Geneva, stands as a tribute to the region's rich legacy.

Château de Ripaille

Originally established as a Carthusian monastery in the 14th century, the Château de Ripaille underwent a makeover into a beautiful house under the patronage of the Dukes of Savoy. Its expansive grounds, featuring groomed gardens, vineyards, and woodland regions, present a compelling blend of natural beauty and human ingenuity.

The château itself features a captivating architectural ensemble, showing numerous styles across its vast history, from medieval origins to Renaissance influences. Visitors are amazed by the delicate features of the façade, the majesty of the courtyards, and the beauty of the interior, furnished with antique furniture, tapestries, and artwork that offer a look into bygone ages.

Beyond its architectural magnificence, the Château de Ripaille possesses a rich cultural past. Its wine-making legacy extends back generations, and the estate continues to produce great wines. Vineyard tours and tastings give an immersive experience, allowing visitors to appreciate the flavors of the region while learning about the winemaking process.

Moreover, the château's expansive grounds serve as a refuge for nature aficionados and history buffs alike. A tranquil stroll through the gardens reveals a rich assortment of plants, while the neighboring forested areas call adventurers to explore their trails and walkways, affording panoramic panoramas of the lake and the Alps beyond.

With its array of fine dining establishments and quaint cafés, Evian-les-Bains offers a delightful culinary experience. Enjoying the best French cuisine while taking in breathtaking views of Lake Geneva and the surrounding mountains is made possible by the town's waterfront location.

Extending your reach beyond the town, the gorgeous area that envelops Evian-les-Bains provides several outdoor pursuits. Trekking paths meander through verdant woodlands and undulating terrain, culminating in expansive vantage places that exhibit the remarkable magnificence of the French Alps.

6

Savoie

S avoie, a charming place tucked away in the French Alps, offers visitors a rich and remarkable experience.

Savoie, referred to as Savoy in English, is a region in eastern France that shares borders with Switzerland and Italy. It was formerly a sovereign nation before France annexed it in the 19th century. Savoie and Haute-Savoie, the two departments that make up the region today, each have their distinct charms and attractions. (We explored Haute-Savoie in the previous section). Now we are exploring Savoie. Again, come with me for another amazing journey!

Chambery

The Savoie region's historic capital, Chambery, has a wealth of centuries' worth of folklore. With its cobblestone streets and well-preserved medieval architecture, entering the village is like traveling back in time. You'll come across striking landmarks like the Château des ducs du Savoie, which was once home to the Dukes of Savoy, as you stroll around the ancient town. Both fans of architecture and history will be enthralled by the château's unique round towers and exquisite details.

Château des ducs du Savoie

Chambery's closeness to the Alps is one of its most alluring features. The town is a great place for environment lovers and adventure seekers to start because it is surrounded by beautiful mountains. In the winter, Chambery serves as a starting point for visits to the neighboring ski resorts, drawing in skiers and snowboarders who are itching to hit the slopes. The surrounding landscapes become a hiker's and cyclist's paradise in the summer when peace seekers seek it out.

The lively alleys and colorful squares of Chambery are its heart. A well-liked meeting place, Place Saint-Léger is crowded with eaties that overflow into the plaza. It's the ideal spot to people-watch and savor some regional food. Don't forget to sample some fondue or raclette, which are regional specialties that capture the essence of the mountains.

Don't miss the bustling local markets, where you can peruse handcrafted items and eat native specialties, for a more authentic experience. It's especially recommended to visit the Saturday market, which provides a genuine sense of Savoie's tastes as well as an opportunity to mingle with amiable people.

Additionally, Chambery is proud of its cultural and intellectual legacy. The University of Savoie, which is located in the town, gives the vibe a youthful energy. The town's creative energy is highlighted by the animated talks and artistic performances you'll witness students having while strolling around the streets.

The variety of galleries and institutions dotted around Chambery will appeal to art lovers. The Musée Savoisien explores the history and customs of the region, while the Musée des Beaux-Arts has an amazing collection of sculptures and paintings from different eras. These hubs of culture offer an insight into the essence of Savoie and its inhabitants.

Let us now discuss Chambery's festive side! The town celebrates everything from modern art to local folklore with a plethora of festivals and events held all year long. The "Fête des Éléphants" (Festival of the Elephants), which honors the town's connection to these magnificent animals, is one event that stands out. Giant mechanical elephants parade through the streets during this festival.

Not to be forgotten are the renowned wines of the area. Savoie is known for producing some very fine wines, such as the Mondeuse reds and the Apremont and Chignin whites. In Chambery, wine tasting is a lovely experience, particularly when paired with a plate of local cheeses.

Aix-les-Bains

This picturesque location, which is on the eastern edge of France's largest natural lake, Lake Bourget, has long been renowned for its healing thermal springs. Aix-les-Bains is a genuinely enchanting destination because it provides the ideal fusion of historical legacy, breathtaking scenery, and decadent activities.

The town was formerly known as Aquae Allobrogum and its history began in the Roman era. The thermal springs of Aix-les-Bains were initially identified as medicinal by the Romans, and their influence can still be seen today as one of Europe's top spa destinations.

Aix-les-Bains's spa clinics and thermal baths are without a doubt its greatest attractions. The town is a refuge for people looking to unwind and rejuvenate because of its warm, mineral-rich waters, which are thought to have therapeutic qualities. In addition to massages and other wellness services, guests at the Thermes Nationaux d'Aix-les-Bains can relax in thermal pools, saunas, and other spa facilities.

Stretching out before Aix-les-Bains, Lake Bourget is a captivating expanse of beautiful, blue waters encircled by rich vegetation and magnificent mountains. There are lots of options for swimming, kayaking, and leisurely boat rides at the lake, which is a must-see. The lake's beaches offer the ideal location for picnics and sunbathing while taking in the breath-inspiring scenery.

Lake Bourget

Explore the many treasures that Aix-les-Bains has to offer for people who have a fondness for history and culture. The medieval stronghold known as Château de la Roche du Roi is built atop a rocky outcrop above the town and offers expansive views of Lake Bourget and the surroundings. Situated on the western banks of the lake, the magnificent Cistercian abbey known as the Abbaye d'Hautecombe is the last resting place for members of the House of Savoy.

As seen by its exquisite promenades and attractive buildings, Aix-les-Bains proudly embraces its Belle Époque past. Enjoy the vibrant city core of the town with its wide selection of stores, cafés, and restaurants serving delicious Savoyard food and wines from neighboring vineyards.

The town's numerous celebrations and events showcase its passion for art and culture. All year long, Aix-les-Bains is home to a thriving calendar of cultural events that includes everything from local markets and art exhibitions to theatrical productions and concerts.

With so much to do in the stunning surrounding natural settings, Aix-les-Bains is also a haven for outdoor enthusiasts. Hiking routes wind through beautiful terrain in the neighboring Bauges Regional Nature Park, providing panoramic views of the surrounding valleys and mountains.

Winter sports lovers will find the town to be a perfect location during the colder months due to its proximity to the French Alps. Many easily accessible ski resorts provide top-notch skiing, snowboarding, and other winter sports.

Foodies will be thrilled with Aix-les-Bains's culinary options. The town's restaurant menus feature regional specialties including diets (local sausages), raclette, and tartiflette, which highlight the flavors of the Savoyard region. The weekly market in the town center is a great location to try and buy regional produce and handcrafted goods.

In addition, Aix-les-Bains organizes several occasions to honor its goods. One such occasion is the Fête des Saveurs, a celebration that highlights local wines and specialties.

Albertville

Albertville, which is also in the Savoie region, saw a significant turning point in its history in 1992 when it was chosen to host the 16th Winter Olympic Games. As you stroll around the town's streets, you can't help but feel excited and proud about its continued Olympic tradition.

The charming city core of Albertville has a cozy, inviting vibe. There are colorful facades, boutique stores, and cozy cafés lining the cobblestone streets and picturesque squares. It's the ideal location for taking a stroll and taking in the gorgeous scenery and small-town atmosphere.

The medieval Conflans quarter, a well-preserved neighborhood with winding alleyways and historic houses dating to the fourteenth century, is one of Albertville's attractions. It feels like going back in time to stroll around this historic district, and you can't help but wonder what stories these ancient walls could conceal.

A part of the Conflans Quarter

Albertville's dynamic character is demonstrated by its diverse cultural scene. The town celebrates everything from local customs and cuisine to music and the arts with some annual events and festivals. A particularly interesting time to visit is during the "Fête des Médievales," a medieval festival when the town is transformed into a bustling medieval fair with artisan marketplaces, fascinating shows that take you back to the Middle Ages, and costumed performers.

Nestled in the heart of the French Alps, Albertville is a winter sports enthusiast's dream come true. The town is ideally situated to explore neighboring ski resorts, including Les Trois Vallées, one of the biggest ski areas in the world, as it is surrounded by breathtaking mountain ranges. There are slopes and paths for all ability levels, whether you're an experienced skier or a novice snowboarder.

The alpine sceneries become a hiker's and nature lover's dream during the summer months. Numerous beautiful hiking paths may be found in the neighboring Beaufortain and Bauges Regional Nature Parks. These trails lead through verdant forests, past tumbling waterfalls, and up to spectacular viewpoints with expansive views of the surrounding mountains.

Enjoy delicious local cheeses, artisanal crafts, a wide selection of fresh produce, and much more at Albertville's weekly market. It's a wonderful chance to interact with the locals and take in the genuine charm of the town.

The Château de Manuel, a stunning 19th-century castle with a view of the town, is another treasure in Albertville. The museum housed in the château offers an intriguing look into Albertville's past by showcasing the town's history and legacy.

Because of its position, Albertville is a great place to start exploring other surrounding sites. Accessible are the immaculate Lake Annecy beaches, the charming town of Annecy, and the breathtaking Vanoise National Park scenery.

7

Isère

The department of Isère, which is located in the Auvergne-Rhône-Alpes area of southeast France, is a fascinating and varied place that provides visitors with a variety of experiences. This region, which gets its name from the Isère River that flows through it, is known for its breathtaking Alpine scenery, quaint villages, and energetic cities. We'll talk about this region's gems below.

Alpe d'Huez

Alpe d'Huez, also known as just "L'Alpe," is a well-known ski resort and mountain community situated in the French Alps' Isère department. With its stunning panoramic views of the surrounding mountains and its altitude of around 1,860 meters (6,100 feet), Alpe d'Huez is a well-liked location for winter sports fans as well as summer travelers.

Alpe d'Huez's winter season is a magnificent time of year when the resort is transformed into a wintry paradise. With access to almost 250 kilometers (155 miles) of ski slopes, it offers a high-altitude ski region that accommodates all skill levels of skiers and snowboarders. With an average of 300 sunny days annually, the resort is well-known for its sunny demeanor, which has led to its nickname, "L'Île au Soleil," or "The Island in the Sun." It is therefore a favorite among those looking for the ideal fusion of superb skiing conditions and bright, blue skies.

The Sarenne run, the world's longest black ski slope at over 16 kilometers (10 miles) with a vertical drop of around 2,200 meters (7,200 feet), is one of Alpe d'Huez's most recognizable characteristics. Skiers with experience should definitely try the exhilarating and beautiful descent it offers. The resort has many moderate slopes and well-kept pistes for novice and intermediate skiers.

Apart from the classic alpine skiing, Alpe d'Huez offers a multitude of winter sports. Cross-country skiing, snowshoeing, and snowmobiling are well-liked substitutes for individuals looking for new ways to explore the areas blanketed with snow. The resort offers snowboarders top-notch amenities as well, including as half-pipes and terrain parks.

Alpe d'Huez is a place that has appeal all year round, even outside of the winter. Hikers and mountain bikers find a verdant playground in the mountainous landscape when the snow melts and spring approaches. With the ski lifts at the resort customized for mountain biking, cyclists can enjoy exhilarating cross-country and downhill paths.

Road bikers consider Alpe d'Huez to be a legendary location. It is a well-known stage in the Tour de France and has come to represent difficult hills and outstanding cycling accomplishments. Over 13.8 kilometers (8.6 miles) and 21 switchbacks, the ascent to the resort reaches an altitude of 1,860 meters (6,100 feet). Many cyclists travel from all over the world to this well-known route to test their talents.

Alpe d'Huez, a mountain community, with a quaint and welcoming ambience all its own. It combines contemporary conveniences with traditional Alpine architecture. Shopping for mementos and winter gear, dining at authentic restaurants, and engaging in après-ski activities are all possible along the bustling Avenue des Jeux in the city center.

The resort also has first-rate recreational and wellness amenities. After a long day on the slopes or trails, visitors can relax and revitalize in spas and wellness centers, which are ideal for relieving sore muscles. There's also a sports complex with an ice rink, an indoor pool, and exercise centers.

Alpe d'Huez hosts a range of festivals and events all year long. Ski and snowboard races are held in the winter, and outdoor sporting events, music festivals, and cultural events take place in the summer.

Alpe d'Huez is a great option for families and anyone looking for an Alpine getaway, in addition to being a well-liked resort for serious skiers and snowboarders. Whatever the season, the resort's plenty of activities, stunning surroundings, and friendly atmosphere make it a memorable trip.

Grenoble

Grenoble is a great place for outdoor enthusiasts and nature lovers because it is tucked away among gorgeous mountains. The Belledonne, Chartreuse, and Vercors mountain ranges around the city, offering breathtaking vistas and countless chances for a variety of outdoor activities all year long.

When you visit Grenoble, one of the first things you'll notice is how well-integrated its modern infrastructure and historic buildings are. The city's ancient origins are evident in its enchanting old town, which features tiny cobblestone streets, vibrant facades, and picturesque squares. There are lots of cafes, restaurants, and shops to be found as you walk about the streets, which contribute to the lively and friendly environment.

Situated on a hill with a stunning view of the city, the Fort de la Bastille is a must-see landmark in Grenoble.

The well-known "Bubbles" cable car, which provides an exciting trip and breathtaking views of Grenoble and the surrounding mountains, can be used to get there. You'll be rewarded with really stunning panoramic views once you reach the summit.

Additionally, the city has a number of top-notch museums, making it ideal for anyone with an interest in science, art, or history. Picasso, Monet, and Gauguin are just a few of the well-known artists whose works may be found in the Musée de Grenoble's remarkable collection. The Musée de la Viscose provides a fascinating look into the past of textile production for science aficionados.

Grenoble has a thriving cultural environment that extends beyond its museums. The city celebrates music, theater, film, and other media with a number of events and festivals held throughout the year. The Grenoble Street Art Fest is one of the most well-known occasions, where gifted artists from all over the world turn the city's walls into enthralling outdoor galleries.

Grenoble offers much for sports enthusiasts to keep them occupied as well. Because of its close vicinity to top-notch ski resorts in the surrounding mountains, the city is a well-liked travel destination for those who enjoy winter sports. Summertime in the area provides great hiking, mountain biking, and rock climbing for all skill levels of adventurers.

In terms of food, Grenoble is renowned for its filling and delectable Alpine cuisine. Don't pass up the opportunity to sample the "Gratin dauphinois," a cheese-baked, creamy potato dish that is a local favorite. Fresh food abounds in the city's markets, and you can also pick up some local cheeses and cured meats for a picnic in the great outdoors.

Grenoble is a university town as well, which gives its streets a vibrant, young vibe. The city's vibrant nightlife, which features a wide variety of pubs and clubs to suit all preferences, is enhanced by the diverse student body.

Les Deux Alpes

Les Deux Alpes, sometimes known as "Les 2 Alpes," is a well-known alpine town and ski resort situated in the French Alps' Isère province. Nestled between the Oisans mountain and the Ecrins National Park, Les Deux Alpes is a popular destination all year round due to its stunning vistas, exciting outdoor activities, and vibrant atmosphere. It is located at an altitude of around 1,650 meters (5,413 feet).

Les Deux Alpes, being one of the oldest ski resorts in France, has a lengthy history that dates back to the late 1920s when the first skiers started exploring the region's slopes. With its extensive and diverse ski terrain, the resort has developed into a top-tier destination that appeals to skiers of all skill levels.

Les Deux Alpes has an excellent ski area with over 220 kilometers (137 miles) of designated ski slopes for the winter season. Because of the resort's high altitude, skiing is feasible from early

December to late April, with exceptional snow conditions guaranteed throughout the season. With plenty of easy beginning slopes, tough black routes for experienced skiers, and massive off-piste terrain for thrill-seekers, the enormous ski domain accommodates skiers and snowboarders of all skill levels.

The Glacier, which is reachable by cable car and offers year-round skiing and snowboarding on its snow-sure slopes, is one of Les Deux Alpes' most notable attractions. Les Deux Alpes is a well-liked option for summertime skiers and snowboarders because to its distinctive offer.

In addition to skiing, the resort provides a variety of wintertime activities to keep guests occupied. Among the many activities are ice climbing, snowshoeing, ice skating, and snowmobiling. Even more options exist for the daring, such as hiking on glaciers or taking a helicopter flight to take in the breathtaking Alpine landscape from above.

Les Deux Alpes is also well-known for its exciting nightlife and après-ski culture. After a day on the slopes, guests can enjoy the vibrant environment created by the bars, restaurants, and stores lining Avenue de la Muzelle, the town's main thoroughfare. The resort accommodates a wide variety of interests and preferences, whether your goal is to dance the night away or simply relax with a warm drink by the fireplace.

Les Deux Alpes becomes a summertime adventurer's paradise as the snow melts and the warm weather approaches. Hikers, mountain bikers, and nature lovers have a plethora of options because to the resort's proximity to the Ecrins National Park.

There are lots of routes to discover, ranging from easy strolls in the valley to strenuous mountain hikes that offer breathtaking views to those who complete them.

Les Deux Alpes is regarded by mountain bike fans as one of the best places in Europe to go mountain biking. The ski lifts at the resort are bike-friendly, offering access to an extensive system of cross-country and downhill paths with different degrees of difficulty.

Another exciting summertime activity in Les Deux Alpes is paragliding, which provides an aerial perspective of the magnificent Alpine scenery. The spas and recreational amenities of the resort offer an ideal haven for anyone in search of tranquility and well-being.

Les Deux Alpes holds a number of festivals and events all year long that contribute to the lively vibe of the resort. There's always something going on to keep visitors entertained, from music festivals and sporting events to cultural celebrations.

8

Hautes-Alpes

The enthralling department of Hautes-Alpes is located in southeast France and is well-known for its breath-taking Alpine scenery, quaint towns, and extensive outdoor recreation opportunities. It's a hidden gem that provides the ideal getaway for those who enjoy the outdoors and the great outdoors. The term "Hautes-Alpes," which means "High Alps," accurately describes the department and its high-altitude peaks and mountains. With several well-known ski resorts that draw tourists from all over the world during the snowy season, it's a haven for lovers of winter sports. Skiing, snowboarding, and other winter sports are made in an ideal environment by the snow-capped mountains and immaculate slopes. Come let's explore this breathtaking region!

Serre Chevalier

Located in the Hautes

-Alpes department, Serre Chevalier is a charming and varied ski resort tucked away in the heart of the French Alps. Serre Chevalier, which consists of several quaint mountain villages and a sizable ski region, provides the ideal fusion of classic Alpine charm, breathtaking scenery, and top-notch skiing.

One of France's biggest ski resorts, Serre Chevalier is comprised of four primary villages: Briançon, Chantemerle, Villeneuve, and Monêtier-les-Bains. Every village has its distinct personality, ranging from the laid-back vibe of Monêtier-les-Bains to the historic charm of Briançon with its UNESCO-listed Vauban fortifications.

With more than 250 kilometers (155 miles) of designated ski routes, Serre Chevalier offers a fantastic ski area for all skill levels of snowboarders and skiers. The ski area is well-liked by families, novices, and expert skiers alike since it offers a variety of open slopes, wooded routes, and difficult off-piste terrain.

Serre Chevalier's outstanding snow record is one of its main draws. The resort has enough natural snowfall all winter long because of its high elevation and advantageous geographic location. The resort has also made investments in state-of-the-art snowmaking equipment, guaranteeing ideal skiing conditions even in the milder winters.

Serre Chevalier offers some excellent off-piste options for experienced skiers and snowboarders. The resort draws freeride enthusiasts seeking to experience unexplored powder and demanding descents because of its abundance of ungroomed tracks and easily accessible backcountry routes.

In addition to skiing, Serre Chevalier has a variety of winter sports to accommodate every taste. For visitors looking for different ways to explore the winter beauty, dog sledding, ice climbing, and snowshoeing are popular options. Throughout the season, the resort also offers a variety of thrilling events and activities, such as torchlight descents, snowboard competitions, and lively après-ski get-togethers.

During the warmer months, outdoor enthusiasts looking for summer experiences can find Serre Chevalier to be a playground. The breathtaking alpine scenery in the area makes for an ideal setting for mountain biking, climbing, and hiking. Nearby, the Ecrins National Park has an abundance of hiking routes that lead to beautiful vistas, alpine lakes, and verdant meadows brimming with wildflowers.

The thermal springs near Monêtier-les-Bains are one of Serre Chevalier's distinctive features. After a day of mountain sports, Les Grands Bains du Monêtier is a thermal spa complex where guests may unwind and revitalize in the warm, mineral-rich waters.

The villages of Serre Chevalier provide a multitude of cultural experiences in addition to an abundance of outdoor activities. Every village has its unique appeal, complete with cobblestone streets, classic Alpine buildings, and a cozy, inviting atmosphere. Discovering the local cuisine and handcrafted goods is a great experience when you visit the markets.

Briançon

The French Alps' Hautes-Alpes region is home to the medieval town of Briançon. It is a mesmerizing location that blends a fascinating Alpine atmosphere, breathtaking mountain scenery, and a rich history. Situated around 1,300 meters (4,265 feet) above sea level, Briançon is the highest town in France and is recognized as a UNESCO World Heritage site due to its remarkable history.

The town has a long history, going back to the Roman era in which there is proof of human habitation. Its strategic position at the intersection of major commercial routes and its closeness to Italy has greatly influenced its historical significance.

The remarkable fortifications of Briançon, constructed in the late 17th century by renowned military engineer Vauban, are the city's most notable feature. The fortifications, which still stand as a tribute to Briançon's military and architectural heritage, were built to defend the town and the surrounding area against invasions. It's like traveling back in time to stroll through the defensive walls and explore the cobblestone streets, offering a singular chance to become fully immersed in the town's past.

A prominent feature of Briançon is its walled ancient town, or "Cité Vauban." It is a labyrinth of winding alleyways, quaint squares, and beautifully preserved buildings that highlight the historical architectural style.

Particularly in the summer months, people and tourists congregate around the Place d'Armes, the old town's main plaza, to take in the atmosphere of the cafes and restaurants.

The Fort Vauban, also called the Fort des Salettes, is the jewel in the crown of Briançon's fortifications, providing stunning sweeping views of the surrounding valleys and mountains.

The fort is reachable via a pleasant stroll or a quick shuttle ride, and the effort is repaid with breathtaking views that make it the ideal location for nature enthusiasts and photographers.

Beyond its historical significance, nature lovers and outdoor enthusiasts find refuge in Briançon. Due to the town's central location in the French Alps, a variety of outdoor activities are easily accessible. The good slopes and copious amounts of snowfall at the surrounding ski resorts of Serre Chevalier and Montgenèvre in the wintertime draw skiers and snowboarders. All ability levels, from novices to seasoned thrill-seekers, can enjoy the slopes.

In the summertime, mountain bikers, hikers, and rock climbers can enjoy a variety of activities in and around Briançon. Not far away is the breathtaking Ecrins National Park, one of France's most beautiful national parks with endless hiking trails leading to picturesque viewpoints, glacial lakes, and alpine meadows full of wildflowers.

Les Grands Bains du Monêtier thermal baths are located in Briançon and are a great place to unwind and rejuvenate. With views of the surrounding mountains, the natural hot springs offer a chance to relax and soak in the healing waters rich in minerals.

The Montgenèvre

Situated close to the Italian border in the Hautes-Alpes department of the French Alps, Montgenèvre is a quaint and historic mountain village. A popular destination for both nature lovers and winter sports enthusiasts, Montgenèvre is renowned for its rich history, superb skiing, and picturesque Alpine setting.

The village of Montgenèvre, with its traditional chalet-style architecture and cozy, welcoming ambiance, radiates an authentic Alpine charm. Because it is elevated approximately 1,860 meters (6,102 feet), which guarantees a consistent snow cover throughout the winter, it is a favorite spot for skiers and snowboarders looking for excellent slopes and breathtaking views.

Montgenèvre, one of France's oldest ski resorts, has a long and illustrious history that began in the early 1900s. The resort's ski area is a part of the wider Via Lattea (Milky Way) ski domain, which stretches into Italy, and spans more than 400 kilometers (248 miles). This extensive ski area offers an incredible variety of slopes, catering to skiers and snowboarders of all levels.

The ski area at Montgenèvre has both easy runs for novices and difficult ones for experts. The resort is particularly popular among families, as it provides a safe and welcoming environment for children and beginners to learn and improve their skiing skills.

One of the unique aspects of Montgenèvre is its proximity to Italy. The resort's location near the border allows skiers to take advantage of the cross-border ski opportunities, offering the chance to enjoy the best of both French and Italian slopes in a single skiing holiday. The connection to the Italian ski area enhances the ski experience and adds a touch of international flair to the trip.

For snowboarders, Montgenèvre offers a well-equipped snow-park with various features, including jumps, rails, and boxes, providing a playground for freestyle enthusiasts to show off their skills and tricks.

Beyond skiing and snowboarding, Montgenèvre offers a range of winter activities to enjoy. Snowshoeing, ice skating, and snowmobile rides are just a few of the alternatives available to explore the winter wonderland and experience the mountains from a different perspective.

In addition to its winter allure, Montgenèvre is also a delightful destination during the summer months. The village and its surroundings become a haven for outdoor enthusiasts seeking hiking, mountain biking, and nature walks. The breathtaking landscapes and pristine alpine meadows create an ideal setting for exploration and relaxation.

Montgenèvre is also steeped in history, with evidence of its past dating back to Roman times. The village's strategic location made it an important trading post and a passage through the Alps for various civilizations throughout the ages. Today, visitors can still admire some of the village's historical landmarks, including the Church of Saint-Maurice. Let's talk a bit more about this landmark:

The Church of Saint-Maurice, hidden in the magnificent French Alps, stands as a tribute to history and architectural beauty. This old church, dating back to the 12th century, captivates visitors with its Romanesque splendor and spiritual significance.

Located amid the alpine village of Saint-Maurice-de-Beynost, this religious institution offers a magnificent façade embellished with beautiful stone carvings that depict tales of a bygone period. Its solid walls, worn by time, generate a sense of reverence and awe as visitors approach.

Upon entering inside, one is engulfed by an aura rich in antiquity. The church's interior, with its soaring ceilings and intricate embellishments, transports visitors to an era of workmanship and dedication. Stained glass windows, lighted by the mountain sunlight, shed bright hues upon the ancient stone floors, producing a captivating interplay of light and shadow.

The Church of Saint-Maurice serves not only as a place of prayer but also as a cultural beacon, organizing various events and performances that exhibit the region's rich legacy. Its significance extends beyond religious limits, affording a window into the artistic and architectural skill of its period.

Surrounded by the breathtaking peaks of the French Alps, the cathedral stands as a symbol of resistance against the backdrop of nature's magnificence. Its serene setting promotes introspection and reflection, making it a must-visit for anyone seeking both spiritual enlightenment and architectural marvels in the heart of the Alps.

Visitors to the French Alps would be remiss not to include the Church of Saint-Maurice in their itinerary, as it not only reflects the region's cultural wealth but also offers a tranquil escape amidst the harsh splendor of the mountains.

The village's vibrant atmosphere includes a selection of cozy restaurants, cafes, and bars, where visitors can indulge in traditional Alpine cuisine and warm up with a hot beverage after a day on the slopes or trails.

III

Things to Do in the French Alps

9

Hiking

The vast network of hiking paths in the French Alps accommodates walkers of all skill levels, from novices seeking easy mountain strolls to seasoned travelers seeking strenuous experiences. Trekkers will find this area to be a hiking haven with its breathtaking scenery, alpine meadows, and gorgeous views. Here are a few of the top hiking routes in the French Alps that are suitable for all skill levels.

Easy and Family-Friendly Trails

The picturesque and mild **Lakeside Path (Le Tour du Lac d'Annecy)** encircles the stunning Lake Annecy and offers stunning views of the surrounding mountains and crystal-clear lake. The trail is kid-friendly, well-kept, and provides a pleasant walk in the middle of the forest.

Merlet Animal Park (Parc Animalier de Merlet): This nature park, which is close to Chamonix, has simple walking paths that pass through alpine meadows where guests can see a variety of mountain animals, including marmots, chamois, and ibex. For those who love the outdoors and families, this hike is ideal.

Les Contamines-Montjoie Nature walks: Families and novices alike can enjoy some short nature hikes in the Les Contamines-Montjoie region. The well-marked paths lead you through verdant meadows and forests where you can see the local fauna and take in the peace and quiet of the Alps.

Intermediate Hikes

Aiguillette des Houches: The Chamonix Valley and the Mont Blanc Massif are breathtakingly visible from this intermediate-level trek. The Bellevue cable car station is the starting point of the trail, which ascends through alpine meadows to the Aiguillette Ridge.

Lac Blanc: Hiking to Lac Blanc from the Flegere cable car station provides stunning views of the Mont Blanc range and the recognizable Aiguilles Rouges. Hikers with some expertise can safely navigate this well-marked, moderately demanding trail.

Lake Lauvitel, also known as Lac Lauvitel, is a gorgeous lake that can be reached via a hike in the Ecrins National Park. The track passes through the Vallon de la Selle, providing a scenic route with vistas of snow-capped mountains and glaciers.

Treks that are difficult and advanced

The well-known multi-day Tour du Mont Blanc (TMB) travels through France, Italy, and Switzerland as it circles the Mont Blanc Massif. Hiking 170 kilometers (106 miles) in length, with stunning vistas of the highest peaks in the Alps, is both difficult and rewarding.

Tour de la Vanoise: This round-trip hike through glacier valleys, high-altitude scenery, and mountain passes in Vanoise National Park is difficult but incredibly beautiful. This is an incredible chance to discover the untamed splendor of the Vanoise area.

Don't forget to schedule your hikes based on your expertise and degree of fitness. Always keep an eye on the trail conditions, pack appropriately, and check the weather forecast. For added safety, it's best to hike in a group or with a guide if you're taking on a more difficult trek.

10

Skiing and Snowboarding

To help novices become comfortable on the snow, the French Alps provide some great beginner-focused ski and snowboard resorts with mild slopes, first-rate ski schools, and a welcoming atmosphere. These resorts are an excellent choice for an unforgettable and pleasurable winter vacation, regardless of whether you've ever skied or snowboarded before.

Flaine: Situated in the Haute-Savoie department of the Auvergne-Rhône-Alpes region in southeast France, Flaine is a ski resort in the French Alps. It is located in one of France's largest connected ski resorts, the Grand Massif ski area. The resort is located roughly 30 kilometers (about 19 miles) south of the town of Cluses and roughly 70 kilometers (about 43 miles) east of Geneva, Switzerland. Due to its convenient access to major towns and airports, Flaine is a well-liked resort for skiers and snowboarders worldwide.

Flaine is a popular resort for people who are new to skiing or snowboarding because of its wide, moderate lines and beginner-friendly slopes. The resort's ski schools are well-known for their kind and understanding teachers, who foster a relaxed learning atmosphere where novices can develop their abilities. Beginners will also find Flaine's compact layout and ski-in/ski-out lodging options to be convenient.

La Rosière:

Situated in the Savoie department of the Auvergne-Rhône-Alpes region in southeast France, La Rosière is a ski resort in the French Alps. Situated close to the Italian border, it's a unique place that provides cross-border skiing opportunities. La Rosière is a great option for people looking for a stress-free introduction to skiing or snowboarding because of its well-known laid-back and beginner-friendly atmosphere. Beginners can acquire confidence and enjoy the mountain views on the resort's mild terrain and sunny slopes. La Rosière is also a part of the Espace San Bernardo ski resort, which crosses the French-Italian border and offers novices a distinctive cross-border skiing experience.

Les Deux Alpes: Well-known for its introductory terrain and first-rate ski schools, Les Deux Alpes is a great option for first-time skiers and snowboarders. With the resort's designated learning zones and mild nursery slopes, beginners can advance at their speed. The ski instructors here have a lot of experience instructing beginners, so learning is enjoyable and successful. Beginners can explore the many blue runs that are accessible as they acquire confidence. These runs are an ideal transition to slopes that are more intermediate in difficulty.

Alpe d'Huez: With a range of beginner-friendly slopes and a first-rate ski school, Alpe d'Huez is another ideal resort for first-timers. For those taking their first steps on skis or a snowboard, the resort's beginner zones are kept up properly, featuring magic carpets and mild slopes. Alpe d'Huez is a popular vacation spot for both families and beginners because it also offers a warm and welcoming ambiance.

Morzine: A large variety of beginner-friendly slopes can be found at Morzine, which is a part of the larger Portes du Soleil ski region. Particularly beginner-friendly are the Pleney area's accessible nursery slopes and mild green runs. The resort's ski schools are well-known for their understanding and knowledgeable teachers, which makes it a great option for novices of all ages.

Les Gets: With its mild terrain and welcoming environment, Les Gets is a beautiful resort that is perfect for novices. It is situated in the Portes du Soleil ski area. The resort is a great choice for families and novice skiers or snowboarders because it has designated beginner slopes and learning zones. For first-timers looking for a well-rounded winter experience, Les Gets is a great option because of its picturesque hamlet and array of off-slope activities.

Châtel: Another ski resort in the Portes du Soleil area, Châtel is a great place for beginners who wish to advance fast. The resort offers a wide range of beginning terrain that's ideal for confidence building, including nursery slopes and gentle green runs. The ski schools in Châtel also put a lot of emphasis on giving newcomers personalized attention and assistance to make sure they have a good learning experience.

Avoriaz: Located in the center of the Portes du Soleil ski resort, Avoriaz has a great beginner park with easy jumps and learning obstacles, as well as a variety of beginner-friendly slopes. The ski schools at the resort offer group and private instruction to accommodate varying learning styles, with a special emphasis on beginner-friendly programs.

11

Mountain Biking

L et's explore some of this gorgeous region's renowned mountain bike routes.

Megavalanche - Alpe d'Huez: One of the world's most well-known downhill competitions, the Megavalanche draws competitors from all over the world. The trail begins at the 3,300-meter (10,827-foot) Pic Blanc summit, which is reachable by cable car. From there, cyclists drop over swift and tricky stretches over 2,500 meters (8,202 feet), passing through alpine meadows and rocky terrain. The village of Allemont, where the event concludes, offers a demanding and remarkable mountain riding experience.

Chamonix Valley: Known for its mountaineering prowess, Chamonix also provides fantastic mountain bike experiences. Numerous paths catering to all skill levels may be found in the valley, such as the picturesque "Balcon du Mont-Blanc" path that offers stunning vistas of the Mont Blanc mountain range. The "Brévent-Flégère" downhill track provides difficult parts and challenging features for experienced riders.

Les Gets Bike Park: With a wide variety of terrain suitable for riders of all skill levels, Les Gets is a well-known mountain biking destination. The world's top riders compete on the legendary "Les Gets World Cup" trail, one of the bike park's several downhill tracks. Berms, jumps, drops, and technical aspects are available to riders, offering an exhilarating trip in stunning alpine environment.

Portes du Soleil: Comprising multiple French and Swiss resorts, the Portes du Soleil is one of the world's largest connected mountain riding complexes. With more than 600 kilometers (373 miles) of designated trails, bikers of all skill levels can find something to enjoy in this area. The network of trails features incredible cross-border bike rides, including the "Pass'Portes du Soleil," which offer the chance to combine the best mountain riding experiences from both nations into one trip.

La Grave: For a remarkable and distinctive mountain riding experience, head to La Grave. After ascending 3,200 meters (10,498 feet) to the Col des Ruillans via a lift-assisted path, riders experience an exhilarating descent that offers views of the recognizable La Meije peak. Because of the rough and difficult terrain, experienced riders looking for an adrenaline rush and beautiful scenery will love it.

Morzine is a popular destination for mountain bikers, offering a wide variety of trails and a vibrant culture. There is a sizable bike park in the neighborhood with well-kept downhill trails, such as the well-known "Pleney" path. A variety of enduro and cross-country trails can be accessed by the "Super Morzine" lift, which makes Morzine a great place for riders who want to experience a variety of terrain.

Bike Park at Tignes & Val d'Isère: Tignes and Val d'Isère are well-known mountain riding destinations with a bike park that welcomes riders of all skill levels. The park offers enduro routes, freeride areas, and downhill tracks. The bike park's flow trails and jumps offers gravity enthusiasts an amazing experience, while the "Tignes-Val d'Isère Enduro Trails" offer a superb blend of alpine vistas and technical riding.

Les Arcs, located in Bourg-Saint-Maurice, is home to a vast network of mountain bike trails, one of which being the well-known "Mont Jovet" descent. Beginning at an elevation of around 2,100 meters (6,890 feet), the track leads riders on an exhilarating drop of 1,500 meters (4,921 feet) that offers breathtaking views of the Tarentaise Valley. For cyclists of all skill levels, the area is a great destination because it offers a variety of other paths.

12

Paragliding

Some of the most breathtaking and thrilling paragliding experiences in the world can be found in the French Alps. Understandably, paragliders swarm to this area for incredible rides with its magnificent mountains, unobstructed skies, and stunning scenery. Let's investigate a few of the best places in the French Alps for paragliding:

Chamonix: Paragliding is among the many outdoor activities available in this well-known destination. Plan Praz and Brévent, two of the valley's take-off locations, give breathtaking views of the surrounding peaks and the Mont Blanc massif. Chamonix provides an amazing paragliding experience, regardless of your level of experience—whether you're a novice on a tandem flight or an expert looking for thermals.

Annecy: Known as the "Venice of the Alps" due to its breath-taking lake, Annecy is a well-liked paragliding destination with excellent thermals and consistent weather. Breathtaking views of Lake Annecy and the surrounding mountains can be seen from the launch locations at Col de la Forclaz and Planfait. The yearly "Icare Cup" paragliding competition, which draws pilots from all over the world, is another event held in Annecy.

Val d'Isère/Tignes: In the summer, the Espace Killy ski area transforms into a paragliding haven. The breathtaking alpine landscape, featuring verdant valleys and snow-capped peaks, is perfect for both solo and tandem flights. Bellevarde and Grande Motte summit takeoffs offer an exhilarating paragliding experience.

Near Grenoble, **Saint-Hilaire du Touvet/Lumbini** is well-known for hosting the Coupe Icare, one of the biggest paragliding competitions worldwide. Dent de Crolles and Mont Granier are only two of the many take-off locations in this area, which provide great flying conditions and stunning views of the Chartreuse Regional Nature Park.

Gérardmer: Situated in the heart of the Vosges Mountains, Gérardmer provides breathtaking views of the surrounding lakes and forests from its attractive paragliding spots. There are options for both thermally and soaring flights from the launch locations at La Mauselaine and Drumont.

Megeve: Takeoffs are from Rochebrune and Mont d'Arbois, providing an amazing paragliding experience. Beautiful views of the Mont Blanc mountain range and the charming village of Megeve below are available from the flights. Expert paragliders are familiar with the thermals in this area.

Valloire: The Maurienne Valley's picturesque mountain hamlet provides ideal paragliding conditions. With its stunning views of the surrounding peaks, the take-off from Crêt du Quart is a favorite place for tandem flights and expert pilots alike.

Grenoble: The French Alps' capital city is home to some top-notch paragliding locations. For thrilling flights over the city and surrounding countryside, there are plenty of launch sites available in the neighboring mountain ranges of Chartreuse and Vercors.

It is vital to remember that paragliding is an exciting and possibly dangerous sport. If you intend to fly alone, you must obtain the necessary training and certification or you must fly with experienced and certified pilots. Before starting a paragliding experience, always check the forecast and conditions as the weather in the Alps can change suddenly.

13

White Water Rafting and Kayaking

White water rafting is an exhilarating activity that will increase your blood pressure and heart rate. The French Alps provide lots of rivers and rapids for rafting lovers of all ability levels, from beginners to seasoned pros. If this is new to you, don't worry! There are several guided tours available, all of which are supervised by experienced instructors who will make sure your time on the water is enjoyable and safe. You'll get a new viewpoint on the stunning alpine landscape while riding the rapids, with glistening peaks and verdant forests serving as a stunning backdrop. The icy waters of the snow-capped mountains will refresh you as you traverse the river's turns and turns, creating treasured experiences with friends or other adventurers.

Now let's talk about kayaking! If you want a more intimate, private contact with the water, kayaking in the French Alps is a terrific option. Riding a motorcycle around serene lakes or down exhilarating rivers is the best way to feel at one with nature. Similar to rafting, kayaking allows you to be in charge of your route and direction. It's a fantastic chance to explore uncharted territory in the Alps and gain access to areas that are often off-limits to larger vehicles or boats. The thrill of successfully negotiating the river currents contrasts beautifully with the tranquility of the lakes, giving you a balanced taste of both tranquility and adventure.

Whether you wish to do white water rafting or kayaking, safety comes paramount at all times. Select reputable companies for tours or rentals that provide well-trained guides and clean equipment. They will not only make sure you're secure but also enrich your trip with interesting anecdotes and background information on history and culture. As you go with the flow, don't forget to pack a waterproof camera, a hat, and sunscreen to capture those magical moments in this breathtaking alpine setting.

Certain water activities work best at different periods of the year. The ideal times to do white water rafting are in the spring and early summer when the snow melts and fills the rivers, creating more exciting rapids and greater water levels. On the other hand, due to the pleasant temperatures and more enticing lakes for a leisurely paddle, kayaking is an excellent summertime sport.

Beyond the thrill of the sports themselves, these experiences allow you to connect with the French Alps' natural beauty on a deeper level. Look out for the wide variety of flora and fauna that inhabit these mountains as you float by. There is so much wildlife in the region. See otters playing or eagles swoop overhead, and your excursion could become even more spectacular.

Here are some great places to go kayaking and white-water rafting:

Isère River - : The Isère River is a thrilling place to go white water rafting. Because of its challenging rapids and pure waters, it's perfect for thrill-seekers seeking an exciting encounter. You'll never forget this unforgettable journey through quaint towns and breathtaking landscapes.

Arve River : The Arve River in the French Alps is a great location for kayaking. Beginning in Chamonix, paddle your way through the shimmering waters while admiring the amazing mountain views. You'll be so excited about navigating through the rapids that your heart will undoubtedly be racing!

Durance River : The Durance River is a popular destination for kayakers and whitewater rafters. This river, near Embrun, has fast-moving water and thrilling rapids. The picturesque surroundings of the Ecrins National Park add even more charm to the adventure.

Dranse River : For an exhilarating white water rafting experience, head to the nearby Dranse River in Morzine. The river offers a range of difficulty levels, making it ideal for families, beginners, and experienced rafters alike. The lush surroundings and refreshing mountain streams make this place even more appealing.

Verdon Gorge : For an incredibly beautiful kayaking adventure, head to the Verdon Gorge, which lies near Castellane. This place, sometimes referred to as the "Grand Canyon of Europe," offers a unique and challenging kayaking experience. It's rather amazing to see the streams with their vibrant hues winding amongst the dramatic limestone cliffs.

Lac d'Annecy: For a more laid-back kayaking experience, head to the stunning Lake Annecy. The Alps and their turquoise waters provide a magnificent sight for kayakers. Paddle at your own pace, find uncharted nooks, and take in the breathtaking scenery.

Giffre River, Sixt-Fer-à-Cheval: The Giffre River offers an exciting white water rafting experience in an idyllic setting. With lush forests and alpine meadows all around, rafters can enjoy the tranquility of the natural world while listening to the river flow.

Romanche River - Le Bourg-d'Oisans: With its mix of serene sections and thrilling rapids, this river is an excellent location for whitewater rafting and kayaking. The path winds through charming communities and offers views of the region's natural beauty.

14

Take A Trip to the Alpine Lakes

Y ou'll be encircled by breathtaking scenery, the towering peaks of the French Alps reflected in glistening waters. Visiting these lakes will leave you in awe of their serene beauty and the stunning sceneries they portray. These lakes are nature's wonders.

1. **Lac d'Annecy**:

First up, we have Lac d'Annecy, one of the most well-known and scenic lakes in the French Alps. This gorgeous lake, which is close to the quaint town of Annecy, has turquoise waters that contrast strikingly with snow-capped mountains. Enjoy a leisurely stroll along the lakefront promenade, go kayaking or pedal boating to get a closer look at the lake, or just find a comfortable place to rest and take in the tranquil atmosphere.

2. **Lac Léman** (Lake Geneva): One of Europe's largest lakes, Lac Léman stretches over the border between France and Switzerland. Charming towns, wineries, and picturesque castles may be found all along its breathtaking coastline. Discover the dynamic city of Geneva and its cultural activities, or take a leisurely boat ride to take in the expansive views of the Alps.

3. **Lac de Serre-Ponçon:**

This artificial lake, located close to Embrun among the mountains, is a striking sight. There are many things to do in Lac de Serre-Ponçon, which is just enormous and offers breathtaking views. You can take a boat excursion to find undiscovered coves and little islands, swim in its cool seas, or even try your hand at sailing or windsurfing.

4. **Lac de Tignes**: An artificial lake close to the Tignes ski resort, this area is a wilderness lover's paradise. The lake's turquoise waters reflect the neighboring peaks in the summer, producing an amazing sight. Savor adventures like kayaking, bungee jumping, and paddleboarding while taking in the breathtaking Alpine landscape.

5. **Lac Blanc:** Hiking to Lac Blanc is a must for those with a greater sense of adventure! Hikers who venture to this glacial lake, which is close to Chamonix, are rewarded with breathtaking views of Mont Blanc and the surrounding peaks. The strenuous hike will be repaid with an incredible alpine experience, making every step worthwhile.

6. **Lac du Bourget:** The biggest naturally occurring lake in France, Lac du Bourget is situated close to Aix-les-Bains. Encircled by verdant hills and vineyards, it provides a tranquil haven from the busy world outside. The lake is a great place for swimming, picnicking, and sunbathing because of its charming beaches and communities along its borders.

7. **Lac des Confins**: Don't pass up the opportunity to see Lac des Confins if you're around La Clusaz. Nestled between thick forests and alpine meadows, this tranquil lake provides a more private and quiet experience. It is an absolute joy to hike around its coast, and you may even see some wildlife.

15

Museums and Historical Sites

I n addition to their breathtaking natural beauty, the French Alps are known for their rich history and treasury of cultural treasures that are just waiting to be explored. The area has a wealth of options to explore its past, from fascinating museums to historic castles, and well-preserved medieval towns to ancient ruins.

1. **Château de Chillon**:

First up, the Château de Chillon, is one of the most famous historical landmarks in the French Alps. This medieval stronghold, which lies close to Montreux on the banks of Lake Geneva, looks like something from a fairy tale. With a millennium of history behind it, it has seen many significant events that have influenced the history of the area. You'll feel as though you've been transported back in time as you stroll through the castle's hallways, discover the dungeons, and take in the breathtaking views of the surrounding mountains and lake.

2. **Aosta Archaeological Area** - :

For history buffs, the Aosta Archaeological Area is a real treasure, located on the Italian side of the Alps. Known by its other name, Augusta Praetoria Salassorum, this historic Roman town is home to astonishingly intact Roman ruins. A few of the attractions that will transport you to the everyday existence of the Romans who formerly called the area home include the Roman theater, the forum, and the city walls.

3. **Musée de la Romanité** :

Continuing with the Roman historical theme, a visit to Nyon's Musée de la Romanité is highly recommended. The amazing collection of Roman relics on display at this museum sheds light on the daily lives of the Roman settlers in the area. Exhibits including exquisite mosaics and skillfully produced pottery provide a window into the region's prehistoric past.

4. **Old Town of Annecy**:

Let's now turn to a more recent past and explore the quaint Annecy Old Town. The canals, medieval structures, and charming cobblestone alleys transport one back in time. Discover the intriguing history of this charming town by taking a stroll around it, stopping at the Palais de l'Isle, an island stronghold dating back to the 12th century, and exploring the local museums.

5. **La Grave:**
   This is the place to go if you're interested in mining history.

This little community in the mountains used to be a major lead and silver mining hub. You can now learn about the once-thriving industry in the region by seeing the abandoned mining facilities, such as the Mines du Grand Clot.

The area where the Mines du Grand Clot is

6. **Musée de la Résistance et de la Déportation**: Recalling the region's more recent past is emotional when visiting the Musée de la Résistance et de la Déportation in Grenoble. The gallant men and women who battled against the Nazi occupation during World War II are honored in this museum. You'll learn more about the hardships and sacrifices made by the French Resistance through firsthand recollections, images, and artifacts.

7. **Albertville Medieval Town** - is renowned for both its quaint medieval old town and for hosting the 1992 Winter Olympics.

Explore the medieval architecture, meander around the small alleyways, and pay a visit to the Saint-Grat Church, which was built in the fourteenth century.

8. Grenoble's Musée dauphinois:

The Musée dauphinois, back in Grenoble, provides a thorough account of the history, customs, and culture of the area. The displays highlight the evolution of life in the French Alps, spanning from prehistoric times to the present. The museum's historic beauty is enhanced by the fact that it is housed in a former convent.

9. Fort Barraux:

Fort Barraux is an interesting site to see for anyone interested in military history. In the 17th and 18th centuries, this castle was crucial to the defense of the area. You may now explore the immaculately kept fort and take in expansive vistas of the surroundings.

10. **Ecomusée de l'Albanais - Rumilly:** This charming museum in Rumilly is a great place to visit if you're interested in learning about traditional rural living in the French Alps. With displays of traditional crafts, agricultural equipment, and quaint old buildings that offer a window into the past, this outdoor museum honors rural traditions.

IV

Events and Experiences from The Culture

16

Alpine Celebrations

F or both locals and tourists, these Alpine festivals are a lovely celebration of the area's rich cultural legacy and offer a singular, immersive experience. These colorful gatherings highlight the traditions, songs, dances, and delectable food that have been handed down through the years and are an integral part of French Alps culture. Let's explore some of the most fascinating Alpine celebrations that you should not pass up!

Fête des Guides

Renowned for its history of mountaineering, Chamonix celebrates the Fête des Guides, or Festival of Guides, every year. This festival honors the bravery and expertise of climbers and mountain guides. It is typically held in August and features a range of events, including mountaineering exhibitions, processions, ceremonies, and folklore performances. The festival's high point is when the local church blesses climbing gear and ropes, asking for protection for the climbers and guides on their audacious adventures.

Transhumance Festivals at Different Places

Animals that travel between lower valleys and summer pas-tures at high altitudes are known as transhumance. Transhu-mance festivals are held in some French Alps towns and villages, where you can see the spectacle of cows, sheep, and goats being herded along the ancient migration routes. The celebrations feature markets, bands, and delectable food. It's an amazing sight.

Fête de la Saint-Jean -

Various Locations: On June 24th, people across the French Alps celebrate the Fête de la Saint-Jean, also known as the Feast of Saint John. It signifies the summer solstice and the arrival of summer. The celebration features gatherings in public areas, traditional music and dance, and bonfires. In a spirit of togetherness and community, locals and guests gather to celebrate the start of the warmer season.

Alpages Festival - Multiple Locations: This event honors the livestock's annual migration from the French Alps' high mead-ows to their new homes. The celebration, which takes place in late spring or early summer, is known for its vibrant parades that include cows decked up in floral garlands and traditional bells. In addition to sampling delectable alpine fare like tartiflette and raclette made with fresh ingredients from the alpine meadows, you may take part in local dances and music.

Carnival of Nice: This event is not just an Alpine affair, but it is noteworthy for its magnificence and cultural relevance in the area. One of the biggest and most well-known carnivals in the world takes place in February. The streets are alive with laughter and excitement as a result of the carnival's magnificent floats, colorful parades, and costumed characters. The "Battle of Flowers," where locals hurl flowers at the floats to create a fragrant and breathtaking spectacle, is the culmination of the festivities.

Beaufort Cheese Festival - Beaufort: The French Alps are home to the delectable and well-known local specialty, Beaufort Cheese, whose manufacture is rich in history. Typically taking place in July or August, the Festival of Beaufort Cheese honors the craft of cheese-making with parades, cheese tastings, and displays by nearby dairy farmers. You will be able to sample different types of Beaufort cheese, discover how cheese is made, and eat delicious recipes that highlight cheese.

La Braderie : Every October, Annecy hosts the renowned flea market, La Braderie. It may not be a typical alpine celebration, but it's nevertheless a distinctive cultural event that draws both locals and tourists. Locals bargain for the best discounts as they browse the many treasures being sold by merchants throughout the streets, ranging from antiques to vintage goods. You can discover unique goods and get a sense of the local shopping culture at this exciting and busy event.

Christmas Markets at Different Places: The French Alps come alive with quaint Christmas markets during the holiday season. Every town and village is transformed into a wintry paradise complete with festive décor, sparkling lights, and booths selling seasonal fare. Along with artisanal goods and, of course, delectable sweets like gingerbread and mulled wine, you may find handcrafted gifts. The ideal way to take in the charm of the

Alps during the holiday season is to visit the Christmas markets.

A fascinating addition to your cultural experiences in the French Alps, these traditional Alpine festivals provide a view into the region's deeply ingrained customs.

17

Handcrafted goods and local markets

F ind a variety of colorful, lively local markets that eloquently capture the customs and tastes of the area in the heart of the French Alps. These markets are gathering places for locals and tourists to experience the Alpine way of life, more than just stores to buy locally grown food and distinctive goods.

On market days, picture yourself meandering along the cobblestone alleyways of quaint mountain towns, the air heavy with the alluring scent of warm, freshly baked bread, pungent cheeses, and seasonal produce. There are many different types of stalls, and each one has a delicious assortment of local specialties. With options ranging from cured meats and handmade sausages to flavorful herbs and spices, there's something to satisfy every palate.

Handmade crafts, magnificent textiles, and traditional pottery, all created with love and care by talented craftsmen, can be found at the market as you stroll about, interacting with the pleasant vendors and learning about their tales. Never be afraid to start a discussion and discover the fascinating background of their works.

Annecy Market

The Annecy Market, one of the most well-known in the area, offers a wide variety of flavors and colors. Indulge in sweet foods like delectable tarts and macarons, sample the well-known Reblochon cheese, and peruse a variety of crafts, including exquisite wood carvings and exquisite handcrafted jewelry.

The French Alps are a veritable gold mine of artisan skill, with a strong respect for age-old methods that have been handed down through the years. Artists and craftspeople in the area are motivated to create distinctive and significant pieces that are in tune with the natural beauty surrounding them by the region's beautiful vistas and intimate connection to nature.

The Alps are home to a rich tradition of woodworking, where

talented craftspeople create furniture, sculptures, and décor that perfectly embody mountain living. The craftsmanship and attention to detail that go into each piece will astound you.

Furthermore, ceramics and pottery-making have a specific position in Alpine culture. You may see potters creating beautiful bowls, plates, and vases out of clay with skill; these pieces are frequently decorated with patterns derived from the local flora and wildlife.

Traditional textile production is another amazing technique that you will come across. The amount of talent and attention to detail that goes into every item is just amazing, from fashionable apparel to warm woolen blankets and finely embroidered materials.

I suggest visiting some of the nearby workshops to get a true appreciation for these artisan crafts. Here, you can see the artists at work as they passionately and diligently bring their ideas to life. Perhaps you will even get to try your hand at some of these crafts and bring home a one-of-a-kind memento created by your own hands.

You may encounter seasonal fairs and cultural festivals in addition to the regular markets, where craftspeople from various villages come together to exhibit their skills. These gatherings foster a vibrant atmosphere and offer a wonderful chance to engage with the neighborhood.

18

Folklore and Music

The French Alps' traditional music is a mellow fusion of beautiful melodies, meaningful lyrics, and a wide variety of instruments. The Alps' inhabitants have a great bond with their music and use it to communicate their happiness, grief, and closeness to the natural world.

A long wooden horn that creates eerily beautiful sounds, the Alpine horn, also known as the Alphorn, is one of the most recognizable instruments connected to Alpine music. The alpine horn, which was first used by shepherds to communicate over great distances in the Alps, is now played at festivals and other special occasions and is seen as a symbol of Alpine culture.

The accordion is another common traditional instrument that you'll hear; it gives many Alpine tunes and dances a bright, vibrant feel. You can't help but smile when you hear an accordion player play upbeat music at a community event and want to join in on the enjoyment.

In the Alps, vocal music is also highly valued, and choral singing is a vital component of the local way of life. Traditional choirs may be heard singing timeless tunes that have been passed down through the ages, with each song telling a story about love, the natural world, or the pleasures and difficulties of mountain living.

The French Alps are home to an enthralling tapestry of myths, tales, and superstitions that have been passed down through the ages. You'll come across a realm of fantastical animals, valiant characters, and mesmerizing scenery as you explore further into these stories.

Belief in magical creatures and spirits living in the mountains is a common motif in Alpine mythology. One such figure is the "Petit Bonhomme des Montagnes," or Little Mountain Man. According to legend, this tiny, cunning animal prowls the heights, tricking passersby and leaving tracks in the snow.

The White Lady, also known as "Dame Blanche," is another fascinating figure in the local tradition. She is described as a kind ghost who guards the mountains and keeps tourists safe. A glimpse of the White Lady is considered a lucky charm by many.

Agricultural customs and the seasonal cycle are also major themes in French Alps folklore. Festivals and festivities frequently center around significant dates on the agricultural calendar, like crop sowing and harvesting. Exuberant costumes that showcase the region's cultural richness, spectacular processions, and traditional dances are characteristics of these festivals.

The "Transhumance," an age-old custom in which herds of cattle are carried up to the high mountain pastures for the summer grazing season, is one such well-known occurrence. Locals and tourists alike participate in the vibrant parades and celebrations that go along with the cattle's climb as part of this ceremony, which is observed with great passion.

There is also a long history of storytelling in the French Alps. Oral storytelling is sustained by the transmission of stories by elders to future generations, stories of bravery, love, and adventure. In addition to being enjoyable, these tales help to preserve the heritage and morals of Alpine villages.

The dance is one of the most captivating elements of French Alps folklore. Folk dances are a pleasure to behold, with their deft movement and upbeat music. One popular circle dance that is guaranteed to entice you to participate in the fun is the "Rondeau," which is performed during festivals.

19

Culinary Delights!

Y ou'll be treated to a rich and varied gastronomic experience that masterfully combines tradition, regional produce, and the simple love of good food as you travel through the gorgeous mountains and charming valleys.

Let's begin with the cheeses, which are the jewel in the crown of Alpine cuisine! The magnificent variety of cheeses found in the French Alps is well known, with each kind having a distinct flavor and personality. Abondance, Reblochon, Beaufort, and Comté are just a few of the cheeses you will experience; get ready to indulge in a cheese lover's dream.

Beaufort is frequently used to make gratins and fondues, which produce a cozy and satisfying dish because of its smooth texture and nutty flavor. Comté is ideal for snacking or wine matching because of its unique flavor and earthy undertones. And who could resist the indulgent, slightly spicy, and creamy richness of a piece of Reblochon, which is frequently used to make the traditional "Tartiflette" dish?

After a long day of trekking or skiing, Alpine cuisine is renowned for its substantial and satisfying dishes that are ideal for refueling. One such delicacy is "Raclette," which consists of heating a half-wheel of cheese and scraping the molten goodness onto a plate topped with pickles, potatoes, and cured meats. You won't want to miss this delicious and social experience.

The delicacy "Fondue" is also a staple in the Alpine cuisine. It consists of a pot of melted cheese placed in the middle of the table, into which diners dip slices of bread. It's a social supper that should be enjoyed with loved ones or friends to create cherished memories and lots of laughing.

If you're looking for a hearty, alpine supper, try "Tartiflette." This filling gratin will warm you from the inside out. It includes potatoes, onions, lardons (bacon), and Reblochon cheese.

The utilization of fresh and locally sourced ingredients is fundamental to the cuisine of the French Alps. Produce is abundant in the area's lush meadows and fertile valleys, and every mouthful will show a difference in quality and flavor.

A characteristic earthy flavor is added to sauces and omelets by including freshly gathered wild mushrooms. The meal is infused with aromatic notes from alpine herbs like thyme, rosemary, and savory, and the mountain air gives the local game meats, like venison and wild pig, a distinct flavor.

Let's now indulge your sweet taste with some delicious Alpine delights. There is a delicious variety of sweets in the area, ranging from flaky pastries to rich desserts, that will leave you wanting more.

French morning staples "pain au chocolat" and "croissants"

are available in the bakeries of the Alps, where they are expertly baked and buttery. You can have the perfect start to the day when you pair them with a strong cup of coffee.

The blueberry tart known as "Tarte aux Myrtilles" is another dish that you simply must taste. Wild blueberries are plentiful in the French Alps, and this pie highlights their delicious tart flavor with a hint of tartness and a buttery crust.

Enjoy "Fondant au Chocolat," a thick, velvety chocolate cake that melts in your mouth when you cut into it, for a true delight. Dessert lovers and chocolate lovers will be in heaven.

The Alpine region is renowned for its distinctive drinks, which elevate the eating experience. Made from alpine plants, "Génépi" is an herbal liqueur that's frequently savored as a digestif after dinner. Génépi's fragrant and warming qualities make it a cozy way to finish a meal.

Try "Chartreuse," a herbal liqueur made by Carthusian monks in the Chartreuse Mountains, for something a little different. The complex flavors of this green or yellow elixir have been relished for centuries, yet its recipe is still kept a closely guarded secret.

Here are a few top restaurants that offer outstanding eating experiences.

1. **Niurou Steakhouse**: Located at Rue de le poste, lieu-dit le bec rouge, le lac, 73320 Tignes, in the center of a picturesque mountain village, Niurou Steakhouse offers a delectable fusion of modern culinary skills and Alpine heritage. This steakhouse takes great satisfaction in providing delicate, premium cuts of

meat that come from local farms. The food is carefully cooked so that the inherent flavors are highlighted. The air is filled with the mouthwatering aroma of grilled meats as customers enjoy perfectly cooked, juicy steaks. Both casual diners and meat lovers will enjoy the culinary trip that Niurou Steakhouse promises to provide.

2. **Le Rustique:** This gastronomic wonder is located at 61 Avenue de la Muzelle, 38860 Les Deux-Alpes, France. This homey restaurant offers guests a genuine taste of Alpine cuisine and radiates warmth and charm. Showcasing the best locally sourced cheeses and cured meats, Le Rustique specializes in classic Savoyard delicacies like fondue and raclette. After a long day of touring the Alps, the restaurant's warm, inviting atmosphere is ideal for indulging in meaty, comforting cuisine. It is also known for its courteous service.

3. **Sush'ski**: Sush'ski is a welcome surprise to the Alps' culinary scene for those looking for a blend of flavors. It is located in Les Gets.

This inventive restaurant offers a distinctive menu that suits a variety of palates and combines Japanese and Alpine cuisine. Together with locally sourced ingredients, freshly caught fish makes for tasty sushi rolls and sashimi meals that are visually stunning as well. Sush'ski's innovative approach to cooking guarantees an exciting and unique dining experience.

4. **Hors Piste:** The distance between the restaurant and Alpe d'Huez is approximately 2.3 miles. Without sampling Hors Piste's delectable cuisine, a trip to the French Alps would not be complete. Hors Piste, a Michelin-starred restaurant, elevates

cuisine with its sophisticated, artistic presentations and daring flavor combinations. The chefs here create culinary wonders that transcend the bounds of traditional Alpine cuisine by fusing flavors from throughout the world. The result is a sophisticated and elegant symphony of flavors, textures, and scents that will stay with you forever.

5. **Restaurant Les Ronins:** Offering a dining experience that enthralls the senses and the palate, Restaurant Les Ronins is tucked away amid magnificent alpine panoramas. Each dish is a balanced celebration of regional flavors, with an emphasis on using fresh, in-season ingredients. Les Ronins' talented cooks skillfully create classic Alpine cuisine while adding a contemporary flair. With dishes like exquisite mountain fish and traditional rosti, the restaurant's menu honors the region's rich culinary legacy. For any culinary enthusiast visiting the French Alps, Restaurant Les Ronins is a must-visit because of its exquisite décor and kind, welcoming staff.

6. **Source**: Amid the French Alps, Source is a stunning example of sustainability for foodies who care about the environment. This environmentally conscious eatery highlights organic, locally sourced ingredients to highlight the region's bountiful agricultural output. Seasonally driven and creative in its menu offerings, Source dazzles diners with mouthwatering tastes. In addition to being a delightful dining experience, Source is dedicated to helping to preserve the breathtaking natural surroundings.

7. **Le Refuge**: 73150 Val d'Isere, Avenue Olympique is the address of this restaurant. Le Refuge, as its name implies, is

a haven of luxury and comfort for those looking for a break in the breathtaking Alpine scenery. With breathtaking views all around, this alpine eatery serves up a delicious selection of Alpine classics to its patrons. Every dish, from soft game meats to sizzling pots of cheese fondue, is carefully and meticulously prepared. Le Refuge, with its cozy and welcoming atmosphere, invites guests to enjoy life's small joys and take in the splendor of the French Alps.

V

Essential Information

20

Communication and Culture

K nowing and honoring regional customs can improve your trip experience and foster a stronger sense of community in this region rich in history, traditions, and languages.

Naturally, French is the official language of the French Alps. Even though English is widely spoken in large towns and prominent tourist destinations, it's still helpful to grasp some fundamental French expressions and phrases. Even a simple "Bonjour" or "Merci" (Thank you) is appreciated by the locals when visitors try to communicate in their language.

These useful vital French phrases for travelers are as follows:

In the aspect of greetings and being Polite:

- The most popular way to say hello during the day is with the phrase "bonjour" (hello).
- Good evening, or bonsoir, is a greeting that is said to

someone in the evening or after dusk.
- Merci (Thank you) is a short but powerful way to show your appreciation.
- S'il vous plaît (If it's possible, please) - A courteous method of requesting things or asking for help.
- Use the phrase Excusez-moi / Pardon (Excuse me / Pardon) to draw someone's attention or if you unintentionally run into someone.
- Au revoir, which means "goodbye," is a polite word to bid someone farewell.

Simple Questions

- Parlez-vous anglais?(Are you able to speak English?) - Even though many individuals in tourist regions do understand English, it's useful to ask if someone speaks the language.
- Où est...? "Where is...?" is the question. Incorporate the location's name, for example, "Où est la gare?" What location is the train station?
- Combien ça coûte? (What is the price?) - Useful for shopping or pricing inquiries.
- Je me comprends pas (I don't understand) – Say this when something is difficult for you to understand.
- Parlez plus lentement, s'il vous plaît(speak more slowly). If a speaker speaks too quickly for you to understand.

When ordering food and beverages at a restaurant or café, say "une table pour une personne, s'il vous plaît" (one table for one person, please).

Je souhaite… (I wish…) – Say something like "Je voudrais un café, s'il vous plaît" (I would like a coffee, please) while placing your order.

L'addition, s'il vous plaît (The bill, please) – To request the check when you are prepared to pay.

The following sentences will help you when you intend to be courteous: "Bon appétit" (Enjoy your meal) is a polite way to wish someone a happy dinner before they begin.

Congratulations (Félicitations): Use this to congratulate someone.

If there is something for which you need to apologize, say "Je suis désolé(e)"

Remember that the locals will appreciate you even if you try to communicate with them in basic French. The majority of French people are kind and amiable, and they will frequently make an effort to assist you—especially if you appreciate their language and culture.

Directions

À droite (on the right) / À gauche (on the left) – Helpful when giving or receiving directions.

If you're looking for directions to a certain location, use tout droit, which means "straight ahead."

À quelle distance? (How far away is it?) – When you wish to find out how far something is from another place.

Emergency Words and Expressions

Aid moi! (Help!) – If you require assistance when faced with an emergency.

To call the police or an ambulance in the event of a significant emergency or accident, you can say "Appelez la police ou une ambulance."

Regional Expressions and Dialects

You'll come across a wide range of linguistic variants as you journey through this varied region, reflecting the distinct histories, customs, and influences of each locale.

Franco-Provençal, or Arpitan, is the Savoyard dialect spoken in the Savoie region of the French Alps. Some inhabitants in the area still speak this ancient Romance language, which has its roots in the Middle Ages. Even though French is the official language, Savoyard words and phrases may occasionally surface in regular discourse.

"Bonjour" (hello) becomes "Bondjoù," and "Comment ça va?" (how are you?) becomes "Cominté ça va?" in Savoyard. Many of these dialectal terms, like "farto" for "skis" and "grolle" for the wooden cup used to share mulled wine, have roots in traditional Alpine activities.

The Occitan influence can be found in the southern section of the French Alps, specifically in the Alpes-de-Haute-Provence area. Provençal dialect is one of the several dialects of Occitan, a Romance language spoken in southern France.

Phrases that represent the Occitan language history, such as "Adiéu" (Goodbye) and "Benvengut" (Welcome), may be heard in this area. The local French has included certain Occitan vocabulary, enhancing the linguistic diversity of this area.

The Italian language has also impacted the French Alps because of their proximity to Italy. You might observe French and Italian terms and idioms being used interchangeably in places close to the Italian border.

For example, in addition to the conventional French greetings and expressions, you may hear "Ciao" (Hello/Goodbye) and "Grazie" (Thank you) in the Aosta Valley, which is part of the French Alps but is primarily spoken by Italians.

Specialized vocabulary related to mountains has also emerged from the French Alps' varied geography. Local idioms frequently refer to pursuits associated with mountains, such as farming, skiing, and mountaineering.

Although they may not be widespread in colloquial French, words like "cabane" (mountain lodge), "névé" (hard, granular snow), and "bisse" (an irrigation canal for mountain agriculture) are frequent among Alpine villages.

You can come across unusual greetings and statements that are particular to the occasion during traditional festivals and celebrations. These statements frequently draw attention to the area's rich cultural history and capture the festive mood.

For example, you may hear residents referring to certain words and songs at the "Fête des Vignerons," a winegrowers' festival held in the Swiss town of Vevey, close to the French Alps.

Like in any other region, the people in the French Alps have a sense of humor and figurative language that lends character to speech. These idioms frequently depict historical events, the local way of life, and the natural world.

You may hear expressions like "se faire prendre la main dans le sac" (to be caught red-handed) or "être heureux comme un poisson dans l'eau" (to be as joyful as a fish in the water) used in informal conversations.

In France, eating is a fundamental part of the day, and people there take great pride in their culinary customs. Lunch and dinner are typically longer events, so plan time to enjoy the company of people and the local cuisine.

In comparison to certain other countries, tipping is not as customary or liberal as in France. Even though service charges are sometimes included in the bill at restaurants, it's nevertheless traditional to tip slightly if you had excellent treatment.

One important thing to note is that French people are cautious and restrained in public. Be mindful of others and refrain from speaking loudly in public, especially in more quiet towns and villages.

When it comes to dress sense, French people dress elegantly and stylishly. It's best to dress formally in more formal settings. Additionally, bring appropriate clothing for trips to places of worship, as some may require modest wear.

Try and verify whether any local holidays or festivals fall on the dates of your trip. Taking part in these cultural events can be a great way to get fully immersed in the customs of the area and make lifelong memories. While at it, always get permission before taking pictures of individuals, especially locals, out of respect for their privacy and cultural customs.

The French Alps are an invaluable piece of the environment. Recognize your influence on the ecosystem by keeping to approved routes, appropriately disposing of waste, and showing consideration for wildlife.

You can effectively connect with the locals by using the following advice:

1. Look for opportunities to engage in the local community through festivals, workshops, and marketplaces. Participating in the locals' cultural events can foster meaningful relationships and a greater comprehension of their way of life.

2. Take into account booking a room at a family-run guesthouse or a traditional lodge. This is a great way to meet people, discover their customs, and eat delicious food created from scratch.

3. Take Part in Guided Tours and Activities. Local guides can provide insightful commentary on the history, culture, and natural beauties of the area.

You can establish constructive relationships with the locals and promote mutual understanding and appreciation by being mindful of language and cultural differences. Recall that traveling is about more than just seeing new sights; it's also about making connections with locals and appreciating their rich cultural diversity.

21

Financial Matters

One of the main expenses you'll incur while traveling to the French Alps is lodging. The area offers accommodations to suit a wide range of budgets, from luxurious resorts and boutique hotels to affordable hostels and holiday homes. Accommodation costs can increase during the busiest ski season, particularly in well-known locations like Chamonix or Val d'Isère, so it's better to book ahead of time to get the best rates.

Another substantial component of your spending is dining. There will be plenty of chances for you to savor the delectable cuisine that the French Alps are famed for. The cost of restaurants and cafes varies; mountain refuges provide basic, budget-friendly meals, but sophisticated dining can be more costly. Try your local markets and grocery stores if you're on a tight budget to obtain fresh vegetables and regional delicacies for a picnic in the gorgeous outdoors.

Let's now discuss transportation. There are several ways to get to the French Alps: you can fly to big cities like Lyon or Geneva, then take a train or bus to the mountain communities. If you want to see a lot of different places, renting a car can be helpful, but be aware that some mountain roads can be difficult to drive, particularly in the winter. It is feasible to move around without a car because many ski resorts offer shuttle services and public transportation is frequently offered.

Winter sports are, of course, a major draw in the French Alps. Because skiing and snowboarding are so popular, lift passes can take up a sizable portion of your budget. For greater value, compare prices and take into account package deals that include lodging and ski passes. Prices vary based on the resort and the length of your stay.

There are lots of outdoor things to do during your summer visit, such as hiking, mountain biking, and paragliding. Include in your budget any costs associated with rental equipment or hiring guides for certain activities. In addition, a lot of national parks and nature reserves have admission fees, which help to fund the upkeep and conservation of these stunning places.

Purchasing presents and souvenirs is an additional factor to take into account. The French Alps provide distinctive goods such as regional handicrafts, delectable cheese, and traditional apparel. Even though it can be tempting to carry souvenirs home, plan your spending to prevent going over budget.

France utilizes the Euro (EUR, €) for payments and currencies. Although most places accept credit and debit cards, it's usually a good idea to have extra cash on hand, particularly in mountainous or smaller towns where card facilities might not be plentiful. The majority of communities have plenty of ATMs where you can take out cash whenever you need it.

Let's talk about tipping etiquette last. Although service costs are typically included in the bill in France, it is customary to leave a little tip (between 5 and 10%) in recognition of excellent service. It's not required, though, and the choice to tip ultimately comes down to how happy you are with the service you received.

You don't have to break the bank to have an amazing trip in the French Alps with careful planning and budgeting.

22

Safety

L et's go over some crucial safety advice to make sure your trip is enjoyable and safe for you.

1. Always check the weather forecast and trail conditions before embarking on any mountain activity, such as hiking, skiing, or snowboarding. Be ready for unforeseen changes in the weather because it can be erratic in the Alps. Tell someone what you're doing and when you expect to return, particularly if you're going somewhere far from home. If you want to maximize your trip and secure your safety during demanding activities, think about hiring a local guide.

2. Some persons may experience altitude sickness as a result of the high altitude in the Alps. Should you encounter symptoms such as headaches, lightheadedness, or dyspnea, reduce your altitude and, if required, seek medical assistance. Drink in moderation and stay hydrated; alcohol can worsen the effects of altitude.

Acute mountain sickness (AMS), another name for altitude sickness, can be a problem while visiting high-altitude locations like the French Alps. It happens when the body can't swiftly adapt to the lower oxygen concentrations at higher altitudes. Precautions against altitude sickness are crucial for a safe and pleasurable journey. Let's talk about some steps you can take to reduce the risk:

A. Gradual Ascent: A very important safety measure is to gradually ascend to greater elevations. Steer clear of abrupt elevation changes as this won't give your body enough time to adjust. Plan your route such that, before arriving at higher locations, there are intermediate pauses at lower elevations, if at all possible.

B. Keep Yourself Hydrated: At high elevations, staying well hydrated is crucial. Drink plenty of water throughout the day, even if you don't feel thirsty.
    Becoming dehydrated can worsen the symptoms of altitude sickness, so always drink plenty of water.

C. Limit Coffee and Alcohol: Dehydration is a risk factor for altitude sickness that can be exacerbated by both coffee and alcohol. You can still enjoy the occasional glass of wine or cup of coffee, but you should balance it out with lots of water.

D. Steer Clear of Strenuous Activities: It's advisable to steer clear of physically demanding activities during the first 24 to 48 hours at a higher altitude. Give your body enough time to adjust before going on strenuous sports or excursions.

E. Rest at Lower Elevations: Try to spend the first night at a lower elevation than what you do during the day. Accommodations at lower elevations are available in many French Alps ski destinations, which might facilitate a more comfortable adjustment for your body.

F. Medications: Some drugs can either prevent or lessen the symptoms of altitude sickness. One drug that is frequently administered that can help with acclimatization is acetazolamide, also known as Diamox. But before taking any drug, always get medical advice, and be mindful of any possible negative effects.

G. Listen to Your Body: Be aware of how your body feels and act quickly to treat any altitude sickness symptoms. Headache, nausea, dizziness, shortness of breath, and exhaustion are typical symptoms. Should you encounter severe symptoms, quickly descend to a lower altitude and, if necessary, seek medical assistance.

H. Steer clear of Smoking: Smoking exacerbates the symptoms of altitude sickness. If you smoke, you might want to cut back or stop altogether while you're at a higher altitude.

I. Eat Foods High in Calorie Content: Your body has to expend more calories to stay energetic at higher elevations. Eat a healthy, well-balanced meal that provides adequate calories to assist your body's altitude adjustment and maintain your energy levels.

J. Acclimate Gradually: Before traveling to higher altitudes, if you have the time, think about acclimating for a day or two at intermediate elevations. The chance of altitude sickness can be greatly decreased using this method.

K. Travel in a Group: It's helpful to travel in a group so that you can watch out for each other's symptoms of altitude sickness. Members of the group can also offer advice and support if somebody feels uncomfortable.

L. Know When to Descend: It's critical to discern when the symptoms of altitude sickness intensify. It is imperative that you or a member of your party immediately descend to a lower altitude if symptoms worsen even after you have rested and hydrated.

2. Skiing and snowboarding: Wear the proper safety equipment, such as goggles and a helmet, if you want to hit the slopes. Be aware of your surroundings and other skiers, as well as the ski resort's rules and regulations. Remain hydrated and take breaks when necessary to prevent exhaustion and injuries.

3. Driving Safety: Keep in mind that some mountain roads can be narrow and steep whether you're renting a car or driving in the French Alps. Be careful when driving, especially in bad weather. Learn how to use snow chains before you go out on your journey, as they may be required in the winter. Stay on approved routes and stay away from detours that could take you to dangerous or unreachable places.

4. Wildlife Encounters: Although there are many different kinds of wildlife in the French Alps, seeing big beasts like chamois or ibex is not very often. If you do encounter any wild creatures,

keep a safe distance from them as it is best to observe them from a distance. For your safety and the protection of the animals, do not feed them or approach them too closely.

5. Sun Protection: Even on overcast days, the sun may be very strong at high elevations. Wear a hat, sunglasses, and sunscreen to protect your skin from UV rays.

Make sure you are properly covered because snow can reflect sunlight and increase your chances of being sunburned.

6. Swimming Safety: Be mindful of the water's temperature and currents if you intend to swim in one of the area's stunning lakes or rivers. Even in the summer, certain lakes that receive their water from mountain streams can be rather cold. For a fun and safe swim, stay in the approved swimming areas and pay attention to warning signs.

7. Avalanche Safety: Be mindful of the possibility of avalanches throughout the winter, particularly if you intend to go off-piste skiing or snowboarding. Always keep an eye on the avalanche prediction and make sure you have the essential safety gear, such as a shovel, probe, and transceiver. Use a certified guide or stay on designated ski runs if you lack experience evaluating avalanche risk.

8. Remain Hydrated and Nourished: Eating regular meals and drinking lots of water can help you stay energized whether you're visiting the area or participating in physical activities. Lack of nutrition and dehydration can negatively impact your general health and enjoyment of the vacation.

9. Emergency Contact Information: Write down or store on your phone the vital phone numbers of your nation's embassy or consulate, as well as the local emergency services. You'll have the information you need on hand in case anything unforeseen happens.

France is included in the European Union's universal emergency number list, which is 112. To contact the police, fire department, or ambulance, dial this number.

To reach SAMU (Service d'Aide Médicale d'Urgence), the French medical emergency services, in the event of a medical emergency, dial 15. They'll send out an ambulance or provide you with phone-based medical advice.

Dial 17 for police help. If you have any non-medical crises or security-related concerns, you can reach the local police services by calling this number.

Call the local fire department (Sapeurs-Pompiers) at 18 to report a fire or to make a service request.

If you require aid or rescue in the mountains, contact the Peloton de Gendarmerie de Haute Montagne (PGHM) at 04 50 53 16 89. They can help in an emergency and are experts at mountain rescues.

You can use any available network to contact emergency services by dialing 112 or 1122 if you're in a location with spotty or nonexistent network connectivity. This is particularly useful in isolated mountainous areas.

As a foreign visitor, get in touch with your home country's embassy or consulate in France if you run into any significant legal problems or need consular help. Having their contact details written down or stored on your phone is a smart idea.

Learn about the laws and customs of the area, especially any unique rules that apply to national parks or other protected places. Be mindful of the environment and wildlife, and dispose of your rubbish properly.

Recall that everyone bears some responsibility for safety. Watch out for your fellow travelers and lend a helping hand to those in need. You may fully appreciate the wonders of the French Alps while guaranteeing a secure and enjoyable trip by being alert and organized.

23

Moving around the French Alps

Navigating the French Alps is a singular and picturesque experience, with its untamed landscape and quaint towns tucked between towering peaks. Let's examine the several modes of transportation that are available to ensure a smooth and pleasurable trip across the Alps.

1. Trains: In addition to being practical, taking a train ride through the French Alps is visually pleasing. The French national railway network (SNCF) provides frequent services to key towns and cities, providing excellent connectivity throughout the region. The Mont Blanc Express is one of the most famous train trips in the Alps; it passes through quaint Alpine communities and attractive valleys and provides breathtaking views of Europe's highest peak, Mont Blanc. The TGV (high-speed train) link between Paris and places like Grenoble, Chambéry, and Annecy is another well-liked route that makes it simple to reach the Alps from the French capital.

2. Buses and Coaches: If you're looking for a dependable way to

get about the French Alps, buses and coaches are a great choice. You may explore the intricacies of this magnificent region by taking advantage of the local bus services that run between cities and villages. Furthermore, major cities and villages are connected by regional coach services, which makes it easy to go to locations that do not have direct train connections.

3. Car Rentals: Hiring a car is a common option if you want the flexibility to travel at your speed. With your wheels, you may travel to farther-flung locations, explore off the usual route, and make impromptu stops to soak in breathtaking views. Remember that driving in the highlands can be difficult, particularly during the winter when icy and snow-covered roads may be an issue. But the gorgeous scenery and picturesque driving make it all worthwhile.

4. Cable Cars and Gondolas: These are the best options for taking in the unmatched views of the Alps. With ease, these aerial lifts take you to the top of mountains, where you may enjoy expansive views of the surrounding terrain. These rides offer access to hiking paths, ski slopes, and breathtaking photo ops from the Aiguille du Midi in Chamonix to the Aiguille du Midi in Annecy.

5. Biking and Cycling: Biking is an excellent method to get a close-up look at the region's splendor. The French Alps are a haven for outdoor enthusiasts. The Alps provide cycling opportunities for all skill levels, whether you're a seasoned mountain biker looking for difficult terrain or a leisurely rider taking in stunning rural routes. Numerous cities have bike rentals, and some even have bike lanes specifically designed for fun and safe rides.

6. Walking and Hiking: These activities offer a close-up view of the Alps' breathtaking scenery. There is a vast network of paths in the area that meanders through forests, meadows, and mountain peaks. Everybody can choose a path they enjoy, ranging from easy, one-day strolls to strenuous, multi-day hikes. Keep an eye out for the designated Ge Randonnée) paths, which are routes for long-distance hiking that cross the entire nation.

7. Ski Resort Shuttles: In the winter, ski resort shuttles offer a practical means of transportation between adjacent cities and ski regions. These shuttles provide a stress-free way to move around the mountains, whether you're hitting the slopes or just want to take in the snow-covered beauty.

8. Electric Bikes and Scooters: The popularity of eco-friendly modes of mobility is growing along with environmental consciousness. In the French Alps, several towns and cities have started offering electric bike and scooter rentals, making it an enjoyable and environmentally friendly option to see the area's sights.

9. Ridesharing and carpooling: These applications can be helpful if you want to meet other travelers and reduce your transportation expenses. These services provide an inexpensive and enjoyable means of transportation by matching customers going in the same direction with drivers who have seats available.

10. Horses and Horse-Drawn Carriages: You might encounter horse-drawn carriages in some mountain settlements, which would give your travel options a hint of the past. A distinctive

and nostalgic experience, horse-drawn carriage rides through charming streets and gorgeous scenery.

24

Where to Stay

After discovering the splendors of the French Alps, it's time to talk about something warm and comfortable: lodging! Imagine this: relaxing in a comfortable bed while taking in the tranquil splendor of the Alps following a day of hiking or skiing. You can choose from a wide range of enjoyable lodging options that suit various tastes and price ranges. Now let's get started!

Let's explore the many accommodations that this idyllic paradise has in store for you.

Hotels and Resorts

Oh, lodgings! Here, they are of different forms and sizes. The Alps have it all, from opulent resorts with spa services that will make you feel like a king or queen to cozy, family-run mountain lodges that radiate rustic charm. Luxurious hotels with breathtaking views of Mont Blanc may be found in

Chamonix-Mont-Blanc. A variety of boutique and lakefront hotels that combine contemporary comfort with historical charm can be found in Annecy. We'll examine a few excellent locations to stay in the French Alps.

Among the top five-star establishments in the French Alps are these:

Hotel Pashmina Le Refuge

Situated in the picturesque Val Thorens ski resort in the heart of the French Alps, Hotel Le Pashmina is a picture of elegance in a classic chalet setting. Located around 35 miles from the quaint village of Moûtiers and 6 km from the tranquil Lac du Lou, this elegant hotel provides a scenic haven amidst the wonders of nature.

The hotel offers tastefully furnished rooms with contemporary conveniences including minibars filled with snacks, free Wi-

Fi, and flat-screen TVs. The majority of rooms have balconies with amazing views of the mountains around, which enhances the visitor experience. Upgraded rooms and suites offer large separate living areas and Nespresso machines for guests looking for an extra bit of luxury. Some even go so far as to add the luxury of Turkish baths. The stylish one- to four-bedroom apartments also feature fully functional kitchens, and some of them have jacuzzi baths for added leisure. Remarkably, the hotel also provides a special and comfortable lodging alternative in the form of an opulent geodesic tent with a wood burner.

The hotel provides a delicious complimentary breakfast to get your day started, so your Alpine excursions will get off to a great start. For the comfort of visitors, a convenient village shuttle service is also offered. Two elegant restaurants and a cozy bar that satisfy a range of palates enhance the culinary experience.

In addition to lodging and food, Hotel Le Pashmina offers some alluring extras. Enjoy some downtime in the spa or cool down with a swim in the indoor pool. Maintain your exercise regimen at the well-equipped gym or get ready for your ski vacations at the on-site ski shop.

Hotel Le Pashmina is more than simply a place to stay; it's a sanctuary that meets all of your requirements and wants. This elegant hotel in the heart of the French Alps provides an all-encompassing experience that blends in well with the breathtaking natural surroundings, whether you're looking for an opulent retreat, a gourmet adventure, or daring adventures on the slopes. To learn more, please contact +33 4 79 00 09 99.

b) **Mont-blanc Chamonix Hotel**

The opulent Hotel Mont-Blanc is tucked away in the middle of Chamonix-Mont-Blanc, surrounded by breathtaking mountains and providing convenient access to the Brévent ski lifts, which are only a short 10-minute stroll away.

The hotel offers modern, light-colored rooms with light-wood details that provide a calm ambiance. Modern amenities including free Wi-Fi, satellite TV, and refreshing rainfall showers are included in these rooms. Many of the suites have balconies with breathtaking views of the mountains for added comfort, and some even have private saunas for an added sense of pleasure.

Savor delectable dishes at the hotel's classy French restaurant, which is enhanced with a stylish lounge bar with an alpine feel and outdoor seating that changes seasonally to provide a magical eating atmosphere. Hotel Mont-Blanc has a variety of amenities that are intended to enhance your stay in addition to lodging. Take a dip in the heated outdoor pool or work out in the well-equipped gym. After a full day of alpine adventures, visitors can unwind in the hotel's spa and hot tub for maximum relaxation.

The hotel kindly provides a free shuttle service to adjacent ski slopes to make your skiing adventures even more enjoyable. This ensures convenience and simple access for guests who can't wait to hit the slopes.

The hotel's phone number is +33 4 50 53 05 64.

c) **L'Apogee**

L'Apogee is built on a former Olympic ski jump, distinguishing itself as a seasonal opulent getaway approximately 1.1 km away from Courchevel's town center. Its modest yet exquisite rooms boast woodsy charm, with marble-clad bathrooms, flat-screen TVs, and the possibility of balconies affording breathtaking valley views. The suites improve the experience with lounge areas, steam showers, heated bathroom floors, and the option for additional bedrooms, while the grand 4-bedroom penthouse dazzles with a dining room, whirlpool tub, and a rooftop terrace holding a hot tub. For those seeking a more private stay, chalets are also available.

Guests can enjoy in fine cuisine at the high-end French restaurant supplemented with a sushi counter, along with the appeal of a sophisticated cigar lounge and a fashionable cocktail bar. The hotel also includes an indoor pool, a spa for maximum relaxation, unique boutiques for luxury retail therapy, and a dedicated kids' club for families to enjoy their stay to the fullest. For more inquiries contact +33 4 79 04 01 04.

d) **Hotel Montblanc**

The opulent Hotel Mont-Blanc is tucked away in the middle of Chamonix-Mont-Blanc, surrounded by breathtaking mountains and providing convenient access to the Brévent ski lifts, which are only a short 10-minute stroll away.

The hotel offers modern, light-colored rooms with light-wood details that provide a calm ambiance. Modern amenities including free Wi-Fi, satellite TV, and refreshing rainfall showers are included in these rooms. Many of the suites have balconies with breathtaking views of the mountains for added comfort, and some even have private saunas for an added sense of pleasure.

Savor delectable dishes at the hotel's classy French restaurant, which is enhanced with a stylish lounge bar with an alpine feel and outdoor seating that changes seasonally to provide a magical eating atmosphere. Hotel Mont-Blanc has a variety of amenities that are intended to enhance your stay in addition to lodging. Take a dip in the heated outdoor pool or work out in the well-equipped gym. After a full day of alpine adventures, visitors can unwind in the hotel's spa and hot tub for maximum relaxation.

The hotel kindly provides a free shuttle service to adjacent ski slopes to make your skiing adventures even more enjoyable. This ensures convenience and simple access for guests who can't wait to hit the slopes.

Not only a place to stay, Hotel Mont-Blanc is a haven where elegance and the breathtaking surroundings of Chamonix-Mont-Blanc collide. Offering a wonderful hideaway for guests seeking a memorable Alpine experience, this luxury hotel combines modern comfort with spectacular views and top-notch services. For additional information, please contact +33 4 79 04 01 04.

e) **Grand Hotel des Alpes**:

Tucked away in the center of the town, this opulent hotel is only a short stroll from the Montenvers Mer de Glace train station, around nine minutes. It is also the perfect getaway for mountain lovers and passionate golfers, located just 600 meters from the Le Brévent ski lift and 3.9 kilometers from the Golf Club de Chamonix.

The luxurious and traditional rooms with their elegant wood paneling and marble bathrooms combine comfort and elegance. These rooms come equipped with contemporary conveniences including Wi-Fi, minibars that are stocked, and flat-screen TVs. Additionally, a lot of apartments have balconies with breathtaking views of the spectacular Mont Blanc. The suites provide opulent whirlpool baths and roomy living areas with pull-out sofas for enhanced comfort and convenience for those looking for a little more luxury.

The hotel offers amenities that promote rest and renewal. Take in the peace and quiet in the spa, which has a relaxing hot tub and a welcoming indoor pool. In addition, visitors can take advantage of massage services, steam rooms, and saunas, guaranteeing a genuinely luxurious stay.

A delicious breakfast provided in a light-filled dining area will start your day off well and set the stage for an exciting day ahead. A chic lounge is available for anyone looking to unwind in style. It's the ideal place to unwind and mingle.

The hotel provides a ski-slope shuttle service to further improve guest convenience and guarantee quick access to the neighboring slopes for an exhilarating day of snowboarding and skiing.

For additional information, please contact +33 4 50 55 37 80.

f) **Altapura:**

Altapura is a sophisticated hotel that offers guests an amazing Alpine experience. It is located about 10 kilometers from the Cime de Caron mountain and about 51 kilometers from Réserve naturelle du Plan de Tuéda, nestled amid a lovely ski resort with commanding views of the Alps.

The polished wood design of the hotel's rooms creates an air of sophistication. Modern conveniences including free Wi-Fi, smart TVs, and iPod docks are provided in these rooms for guests' amusement. Upgraded rooms feature stunning views of the mountains for a heightened experience. In addition, the suites include large living areas, and the upgraded suites have extra amenities including loft bedrooms and sofa beds. Although the hotel does not have air conditioning, it is noteworthy that room service is available for the comfort of its patrons.

With its variety of dining alternatives, Altapura accommodates a wide range of gastronomic interests. Visitors can enjoy the chic bar/brasserie or relax at the patio bar. The hotel's stylish restaurant has a patio with stunning views of the mountains, making for an exquisite dining experience that is all the more alluring.

The hotel provides a selection of amenities designed to make your stay in the Alps unforgettable. In addition to a specialized ski concierge and ski storage facilities, guests can reach the property by ski in and out. To further meet diverse leisure and recreational demands, there is a dedicated kids' play area, an outdoor pool, and a fitness club.

Altapura is a doorway to an alpine wonderland, not just a place to rest. This upmarket hotel offers a unique Alpine experience, ideal for savoring the charm of the mountains, with its blend of sophisticated lodgings, a variety of dining options, and a wealth of activities geared for both rest and adventure. For further details, please contact +33 4 80 36 80 36.

Bed & Breakfasts and Guesthouses

Consider booking a room at a quaint bed & breakfast or guest-house for a more individualized experience at a lower cost. Imagine waking up to the aroma of your hosts' handmade pastries and freshly prepared coffee. These lodgings frequently provide a cozy atmosphere, insider knowledge of the area, and home-cooked meals that will make you feel completely at home. Let's examine a few great choices below:

a) **Les Jardins d'Eleusis:**

Located in Murs, this bed and breakfast welcomes pets and

features free WiFi, a sun patio, and a seasonal outdoor pool. It offers a peaceful environment for guests to relax in among the beauty of nature. Free private parking is conveniently available on-site for visitors.

This quaint bed and breakfast offers things to keep guests entertained during their stay, like Nintendo Wii consoles and flat-screen TVs. A fantastic place to unwind after an exciting day of exploring is offered by certain units, which feature comfortable seating areas. Every room has a kettle and coffee maker so that visitors can have their preferred drinks whenever they choose. Guests will find private bathrooms to increase comfort, and robes and slippers are given for an extra touch of elegance.

Upon request, visitors to B&B Les Jardins d'Eleusis can enjoy prepared meals, which offer a wonderful and personalized touch to their stay. The bed and breakfast also provides free bicycle rentals so that visitors can freely explore the neighborhood at their leisure.

To further enhance convenience and leisure, guests can enjoy free drinks from the minibar while still in the comfort of their rooms.

There's more exploring to be done outside the B&B; Aix-en-Provence is 50 kilometers away, and Avignon is only 35 kilometers away. Avignon-Provence Airport is located about 28 kilometers away from the property for guests traveling by air.

The B&B Les Jardins d'Eleusis welcomes visitors to unwind in a tranquil setting while providing a unique combination of luxury, convenience, and attentive service amidst the stunning Murs scenery. The bed & breakfast's phone number is +33 6 78 58 02 26.

b) **La Ferme D'Angele**

A warm country-style B&B in the heart of the gorgeous Alps, La Ferme d'Angele is housed in a quaint stone-and-timber building that dates back to 1830. This charming hideaway is conveniently located 13 kilometers from the La Rosière ski resort and 6 kilometers from the Bourg Saint Maurice rail station. It provides guests with easy access to both exhilarating ski excursions and natural beauties.

The B&B has five comfortable rooms that can each accommodate up to four visitors and are decorated in a pleasant and rustic style. While some rooms have communal toilets, others have the comfort of en suite baths. A separate cottage with a living space complete with a cozy sofa is also offered, providing guests with a more private and customized stay.

Start the day with a delicious breakfast provided in the rustic dining area of the B&B, which has slate floors and a cozy fireplace that creates a cozy atmosphere. If you're looking for a full gastronomic experience, dinner can be ordered.

After a day of exploring or skiing, guests can unwind in the garden area of the B&B or in the soothing waters of the hot tub, which provides a peaceful haven. The terrace offers breathtaking views of the mountains, making it the ideal place to relax and take in the Alpine landscape.

La Ferme d'Angele welcomes visitors to enjoy the tranquil surroundings of the Alps. It is a little refuge distinguished by its rustic appeal, friendly service, and a selection of amenities designed for a calm escape amidst the region's spectacular scenery. For any questions, please call +33 4 79 41 05 71.

c) **Auberge du Clot**:

Located in Névache, about 30 kilometers away from Serre Chevalier, this resort provides quiet gardens and ski-to-door access, making it the ideal Alpine getaway. The facility has a charming bar and a patio for visitors to unwind on, which together create a welcoming atmosphere. For the convenience of visitors, the helpful staff may also help arrange for a shuttle service.

The guest house has thoughtfully provided desks in each room to ensure guests' comfort while visiting. The accommodations are made more peaceful by the seclusion of the individual baths with views of the mountains for each guest. The rooms also have wardrobes, which give visitors plenty of space to store their possessions.

Skiing and cycling are only two of the many sports available in the vicinity of the lodging for those looking for adventure. This region serves to accommodate visitors' varied interests and gives them a chance to explore the stunning surroundings.

Auberge du Clot is also close to other lovely places: Montgenèvre is just 24 kilometers distant, and Le Monêtier-les-Bains is about 34 kilometers away. If visitors are arriving or departing by air, the Oulx train station is conveniently located 44 kilometers away, and Turin Airport is about 133 kilometers from the property. To learn more, please contact +33 4 92 21 18 21.

d) **The Nant**:

Housed in a quaint 1905 farmhouse-turned-chalet, The Nant offers a comfortable alpine-style hotel tucked away at the foot of Mont Chéry. This hotel provides a handy refuge for skiers and those looking for a peaceful Alpine getaway, located just 2 kilometers from the Pléney ski lift, 3 kilometers from the village center, and roughly 91 kilometers from Geneva Airport.

The hotel has uncomplicated wood furnishings in its unpretentious and simple rooms, creating a cozy and friendly ambiance. Different tastes and price ranges are catered for with the choice of communal or en suite bathrooms for guests.

The Nant ensures simple access for guests' skiing experiences by offering free parking and a handy shuttle service to neighboring ski lifts. Meals are available for a fee for anyone who would like to eat on-site. The hotel also has a nice bar with a dartboard and a pool table for entertainment. Visitors can utilize the shared kitchen facilities or unwind in the TV lounge. To further satisfy the needs of outdoor enthusiasts, the hotel offers plenty of room for storing bikes and ski equipment.

With a variety of amenities to make their stay more enjoyable, The Nant welcomes visitors to enjoy a laid-back and comfortable atmosphere. In the stunning surroundings of Mont Chéry, this alpine-style hotel offers a warm sanctuary with its rustic appeal, handy location, and many amenities that cater to both leisure and adventure. The number to call is +44 7478 822278.

e) **Auberge du Fraizier**:

Situated in Thônes, this lodging provides free WiFi and flat-screen TVs to ensure that visitors are connected and amused while visiting.

A cozy dining area and/or a balcony are features of some of the lodging rooms, giving visitors more space and the chance to take in the views from the neighborhood.

The bed and breakfast offers a delicious continental breakfast to its visitors every morning, making for a relaxing start to the day.

The warm terrace of Auberge Du Frazier invites visitors to relax and take in the peaceful ambiance.

A communal lounge room with a tea/coffee maker is available for visitors to use for socializing and leisure, fostering a warm atmosphere where they may enjoy each other's company.

Access to some attractions is made simple by the property's advantageous location. Geneva is around 41 kilometers from the lodging, and Chamonix-Mont-Blanc is about 42 kilometers from the lodging. Travelers may easily reach Chambéry-Savoie Airport, which is conveniently positioned 43 kilometers away from Auberge Du Fraizier. The lodge's phone number is +33 6

37 90 67 88.

f) **La Cle de Bois**:

Situated 13 kilometers from the Oz-Vaujany Ski Resort, La Clé des Bois is a strategically located mountain retreat, nestled in Le Bourg-d'Oisans. Additionally, it's only a 5-minute walk to the Ski Lift, which provides quick access to the well-known Les Deux Alpes ski area. This beautiful B&B has free WiFi available all across the property, a sun patio, and handy ski storage facilities.

La Clé des Bois ensures guests' comfort by providing each room with a private bathroom that comes with free toiletries and bathrobes. A comfortable seating space in certain rooms is the ideal place to relax after a busy day. A patio or balcony is another feature of some rooms, enabling visitors to enjoy the crisp mountain air.

Homemade meals are offered on-site at the B&B, giving visitors the choice of dining in the cozy communal living area or the comfort of their rooms.

Access to the Vaujany ski slopes is made easier for visitors with a free ski shuttle service, making skiing activities in the area more convenient. In addition, visitors may use the on-site sauna for an extra fee, which is ideal for unwinding after a thrilling day of skiing.

La Clé des Bois ensures amusement for visitors with a variety of interests by providing a range of activities, such as skiing and cycling. Additionally, the B&B offers bike rentals for those who want to explore the neighborhood. Notably, Grenoble - Isère Airport, the closest airport, is around 86 kilometers away, and L'Alpe-d'Huez is situated 21 kilometers from the property, offering convenient transit alternatives for visitors. To learn more, call +33 6 08 71 61 02.

g) **Chalet Christine**:
Chalet Christine, which is located in Talloires, provides a tranquil haven for visitors with an indoor pool, spa, and wellness center. The resort offers free WiFi throughout to guarantee connectivity.

For the amusement of its visitors, Chalet Christine offers an iPod dock in each room. Every room has a private bathroom with a shower or bathtub and conveniences like a hair dryer and cozy bathrobes for visitors' comfort. From their accommodations, guests may enjoy amazing views of the mountains and lake, which adds to the experience. For added convenience, a safety deposit box is also offered.

Guests may easily enjoy natural magnificence and recreational activities thanks to the hotel's convenient location, which is only 2.4 kilometers from Lac d'Annecy Golf Course and 100 meters from Annecy Lake. Geneva International Airport Airport is just 53.3 kilometers distant, making it an accessible route for visitors looking for a peaceful getaway at Chalet Christine.

Camping and Glamping

A camping or glamping site in the heart of the alpine landscape is an experience in and of itself. Choose to clamp with all the luxuries or set up a tent next to a peaceful lake. Just picture an opulent tent with a luscious bed and a starry sky above. It's difficult to find the same sense of independence and connection to nature anywhere else as camping does. Campsites come equipped with basic to luxurious amenities, so you may customize your outdoor experience to your preference.

Caravan parks are an excellent option if you would like a little extra luxury and convenience while visiting the French Alps. You can enjoy the great outdoors and have a comfortable home on wheels when you go caravanning. Large plots with electric hookups are usually available in the parks, making it simple to power your caravan and have a comfortable stay.

Caravan parks are perfect for families because they generally provide extra amenities like kid's playgrounds, laundry rooms, and common spaces. They offer a feeling of camaraderie, allowing visitors to meet other like-minded explorers and take their time discovering the mountains.

Being close to nature is one of the main benefits of staying at camping and caravan parks. Numerous of these lodging options are close to well-traveled hiking routes, alpine lakes, and breathtaking vistas. You can get out of your caravan or tent and take a stroll through breathtaking scenery or go on a revitalizing hike.

Being surrounded by nature also increases the likelihood that you will make some animal or avian companions while visiting. Look out for inquisitive animals such as ibex, marmots, and even the elusive chamois. Just keep in mind to view them from a distance and to respect their personal space.

When staying in camping and caravan sites, especially during the busiest times of the year, it's a good idea to make advance plans. Even though being spontaneous can be enjoyable, reservations should be made in advance as popular locations tend to fill up quickly. Additionally, make sure the park's amenities and services suit your requirements and tastes by checking them out.

Packing for a camping or caravan trip should include all the necessities, such as a well-maintained caravan or robust tent, warm sleeping bags, cooking supplies, and, most importantly, a feeling of adventure!

Here are a few that come highly recommended and have beautiful settings along with excellent amenities:

1. **Camping Les Deux Glaciers** (Chamonix): Located in the well-known mountain town of Chamonix. Camping Les Deux Glaciers provides magnificent views of the Massif du Mont Blanc. For those who enjoy the great outdoors, this campsite offers an ideal location for hiking trails, mountaineering, and winter skiing. There is a grocery store, laundry facilities, and hot showers available at the well-kept facilities. You can reach them by phone at +33 4 50 53 15 84.

2. **Camping l'Eden de la Vanoise (Modane)**. It's close to the Vanoise National Park and is a calm, lovely area to stay. Hikers and lovers of the outdoors will find this place ideal, as the location is surrounded by breathtaking mountain scenery. Large sites and contemporary amenities, such as a café providing delectable regional food and a swimming pool, are provided by the campground. Their number is +33 4 79 07 61 81.

3. **Camping Le Panoramic (La Grave):** This 1500-meter-high campsite provides breathtaking sweeping views of La Meije and the neighboring peaks. Because it's close to some of the best climbs and slopes in the area, this campsite is a refuge for mountaineers, hikers, and skiers. The campground is a special and unforgettable option because of its beautiful environment and welcoming ambiance. For additional information, call +33 4 50 52 43 09.

4. **Camping Huttopia Bourg-Saint-Maurice** (Bourg-Saint-Maurice): Camping Huttopia is a great option for people looking for a combination of comfort and nature. This campsite, which is surrounded by a stunning mountain landscape, has large pitches for tents and caravans, as well as glamping tents and

comfortable wooden chalets. The location has a playground, a heated pool, and a comfortable central lodge area for gathering. You can reach them at +33 4 79 07 03 45.

Tips for Choosing the Perfect Stay

1. Consider the location that suits your itinerary. Are you here for the skiing? Look for accommodations close to the slopes. Seeking a peaceful retreat? Opt for places away from the bustling towns. Proximity to activities and attractions matters, so choose wisely!

2. Keep the seasons in mind. Winter accommodations may differ significantly from what's available in summer. Some places might be closed during off-peak seasons, while others might offer seasonal discounts.

3. Immerse yourself in the local culture! Many accommodations offer regional cuisine, activities, or cultural experiences. Look for places that offer cooking classes, wine tastings, or guided tours to delve deeper into the local lifestyle.

So, dear traveler, whether you're seeking luxury, simplicity, or something in between, the French Alps have a snug spot just waiting for you. Get ready to snuggle up in Alpine charm and wake up to the magic of these magnificent mountains!

VI

Day Trips and Excursions

25

Geneva

Situated near the French border in Switzerland, Geneva is a fascinating city worth exploring. It is also known for its global reach, housing numerous organizations such as the Red Cross and the United Nations, which contributes to its distinct multicultural ambiance. With its breathtaking scenery, intriguing history, and varied cultural offerings, Geneva has something to offer tourists of all stripes.

The drive from the French Alps to Geneva may make for a really lovely day trip, as you'll pass through quaint villages, stunning Alpine landscapes, and maybe even catch a sight of the famous Mont Blanc. There are a number of things in Geneva that you simply must see once you get there.

The Jet d'Eau, a stunning fountain on Lake Geneva, is one of the city's best-known monuments.

It creates an amazing image that is visible from many locations across the city when it shoots water 140 meters into the air. Enjoy the fresh air and breathtaking views of the surrounding mountains and lake as you stroll along the lakeside promenade.

The Old Town is a must-visit location for history buffs. Locals refer to this lovely neighborhood as "Vieille Ville," and it is full of cobblestone lanes, old buildings, and cute cafes. You can explore the winding lanes, see St. Pierre Cathedral, and take in the atmosphere of the Middle Ages. Remember to ascend the cathedral's tower to gain a broad perspective of the city and the lake.

The many museums and galleries in Geneva will thrill art and culture enthusiasts. The Patek Philippe Museum features an intriguing assortment of watches from one of Switzerland's most renowned watchmakers, while the Musée d'Art et d'Histoire is home to an extraordinary collection of art, archaeology, and historical relics.

Geneva's food is a delicious blend of cuisines from throughout the world. Enjoy delectable Swiss delicacies like fondue and raclette, or discover a variety of international culinary customs. The city is a great destination to purchase souvenirs because it is also well-known for its exquisite chocolate and expensive Swiss timepieces.

If you have more time, you might like to go on a boat ride around Lake Geneva. It's a great opportunity to unwind and take in the beauty as you drive past charming coastal towns and villages. The adjacent Jura Mountains provide great hiking paths and wintertime skiing and snowboarding for anyone looking for outdoor fun.

Geneva's friendly attitude and cosmopolitan ambiance make it an excellent spot to immerse yourself in the local way of life, even outside of the city's attractions. You'll have a greater understanding of the city's distinct character if you spend some time people-watching at a cafe and engage in discussion with the amiable residents.

Remember, though, that a day trip to Geneva might not be sufficient to completely take advantage of all that the city has to offer. To make the most of your visit, try to prolong your stay to a weekend or longer if at all possible.

With happy recollections of Geneva's beauty, history, and kind hospitality, you'll go back to the French Alps as the day draws to a close. Geneva is a great day trip destination from the

French Alps, whether you're a history buff, a nature lover, or just someone wishing to see a bustling European metropolis.

26

Lausanne

A short hop across the border from the French Alps, Lausanne is a hidden treasure in Switzerland, perched on the banks of Lake Geneva. This dynamic metropolis skillfully combines breathtaking natural beauty, history, and culture, making it the ideal trip destination for those looking for a variety of activities.

The stunning location of Lausanne is the first thing that draws tourists in. With captivating sweeping views of Lake Geneva and the Alps beyond, the city rises sharply from the lakeshore to the nearby hills. The tranquil ambiance created by the beautiful Alps in the distance and the soft sound of the water as you stroll along the waterfront promenade is difficult to resist.

Lausanne's Old Town, which was built during the Middle Ages, is its central area. Charming squares with colorful facades lining centuries-old buildings are crisscrossed by cobblestone streets. With its striking rose window and gothic design, the Cathedral of Notre Dame is a striking structure that provides another viewpoint for taking in the splendor of the city.

The vibrant cultural environment of Lausanne is equally alluring. The many museums and galleries in the city will delight art enthusiasts. Situated on the scenic beaches of Lake Geneva, the Olympic Museum honors the history and ideals of the Olympic Games. It's a must-visit for history buffs and sports fans alike, with interactive exhibitions and captivating displays.

The Olympic Museum

The Collection de l'Art Brut presents original works by self-taught artists, offering a fascinating viewpoint on artistic expression for fans of contemporary art. For those who enjoy photography, the Musée de l'Elysée, which showcases both ancient and modern pieces, is a veritable gold mine.

The energetic student population of Lausanne adds even more

to the city's vibrancy. The city is alive with young energy, being home to the esteemed University of Lausanne as well as other educational institutions. The vibrant markets, bookshops, and charming cafes all add to the vibrant atmosphere of the city.

In Lausanne, foodies' taste buds will dance with delight. The city is home to a wide variety of dining establishments, ranging from chic international bistros serving delectable cuisine from around the globe to classic Swiss cafes providing fondue and raclette. For a genuinely decadent experience, pair your dinner with a glass of Swiss wine or indulge in some of the best Swiss chocolates.

Lausanne's focus on green spaces and effective public transit systems demonstrate the city's commitment to sustainable living. A lovely lakeside walk or a peaceful lunch by the water can be had at the nicely manicured Ouchy Promenade. You can also cool down in the lake by taking a pleasant plunge during the warmer months.

Lausanne serves as an entry point to outdoor activities for individuals in search of adventure. The charming hiking trails among terraced vineyards overlooking the lake can be found in the adjacent Lavaux vineyards, a UNESCO World Heritage site. The adjacent Alps call in the winter when ski resorts for novices and experts alike await.

The summertime Lausanne Festival, or "Lausanne Estivale," is the perfect time to experience the city's exuberant energy. Concerts, outdoor shows, and other cultural events bring the city to life and unite people and visitors in joy.

27

Turin

Situated just south of the French Alps, the intriguing city of Turin, or Torino in Italian, is a perfect day trip destination from the magnificent mountain range. Turin, the Piedmont region's capital, captivates with its dynamic cultural scene, attractive architecture, and rich historical legacy.

Soaring majestically over the Turin skyline, the Mole Antonelliana is one of the city's most recognizable sights.

The Mole Antonelliana in Turin is a captivating architectural marvel that embodies the city's history and artistry. Standing tall at over 550 feet, it was originally intended to be a synagogue but transformed into a symbol of Turin's identity.

Designed by Alessandro Antonelli, the Mole Antonelliana show-cases a stunning blend of neoclassical and eclectic architectural styles. Its intricate details, including the delicate spire crowning its top, contribute to its grandeur. The sheer height and elegance of the structure make it an iconic landmark visible from various vantage points across the city.

Within its walls, the National Museum of Cinema resides, offer-ing a fascinating journey through the history and evolution of cinema. The museum's exhibits, housed in the building's vast interior, feature everything from antique cameras and projec-tors to memorabilia from classic films, making it a paradise for film enthusiasts and history buffs alike.

Ascending the Mole Antonelliana provides visitors with breathtaking panoramic views of Turin and the surrounding Piedmont region. The journey to the top via a glass elevator allows for an immersive experience as the city unfolds beneath, offering a spectacular visual narrative of Turin's urban landscape.

The city of Turin is more than just its breathtaking architecture. The city's stately boulevards, refined squares, and old palaces radiate a classic beauty. The center of the city is Piazza Castello, which is encircled by striking buildings like the Royal Palace of Turin, which was formerly the Savoy royal family's home. A trip to the magnificent baroque palace known as the Palazzo Madama, which is currently the Civic Museum of Ancient Art, provides insight into Turin's historical royal heritage.

The Turin Egyptian Museum has one of the largest collections of Egyptian artifacts outside of Egypt, therefore art fans will be happy there. The museum's artifacts, which include mummies and antiquated sculptures, offer a breathtaking trip through time.

The Shroud of Turin is kept in the Turin Cathedral, which is another important spiritual location. This enigmatic artifact, which some people think is the burial shroud of Jesus Christ, draws both tourists and scholars. Visitors can get a close-up look at this mysterious artifact in the Chapel of the Holy Shroud.

Discover the city's charming cafés and storied chocolate stores, which provide a taste of Turin's delectable cuisine. The city is a chocolate lover's dream come true, especially for its "gianduja," a hazelnut-chocolate spread, and its famous "cioccolata calda," or hot chocolate.

The culinary exploration of Turin continues beyond chocolate. Traditional Piedmontese fare, including the flavorful agnolotti pasta and the delicious truffle-infused treats, is part of the city's rich culinary legacy. Enjoying the food of the area is a must if you want to see the lively culture of the city.

Automobile fans find Turin to be particularly fascinating, even beyond its cultural and culinary offerings. Renowned automakers Fiat and Alfa Romeo are pleased to call the city home. The National Automobile Museum immerses visitors in the development of the automotive industry with its interesting collection of both current and historic cars.

The Po River's banks provide a peaceful haven for a peaceful period at the Parco del Valentino. This gorgeous park is the ideal place to unwind with its lush vegetation and quaint strolling paths.

Turin's lively nightlife comes alive in the evening. There are plenty of taverns, eateries, and live music venues in the bustling Quadrilatero Romano, also known as the Roman Quarter. It's the perfect spot to take in the vibrant atmosphere of the city and socialize with both residents and other tourists.

Although Turin has a lot to offer, the Piedmont region that surrounds it is a veritable gold mine of scenic beauty. Renowned for their hilltop vineyards, the Langhe and Roero districts are home to some of Italy's best wines, including Barolo and Barbaresco. A charming trip from Turin is to explore these picturesque vineyards and taste the regional wines.

28

Conclusion

Y our voyage has been a symphony of stunning scenery,
thrilling adventures, and unforgettable encounters. You
know this even as you wave farewell to the gorgeous
French Alps. From the majestic mountains of Mont Blanc to the
quaint Alpine towns, this area has woven its enchantment and
left a lasting impression on your heart.

We have explored the Alpine beauty in this travel guide, re-
vealing the famous locations and undiscovered treasures that
make the French Alps a must-visit location for all nature lovers
and adventurers. The French Alps welcome you with open
arms, providing an incredible escape from the ordinary, whether
you were looking for heart-pounding sports like skiing and
paragliding or you just wanted peace and quiet in the middle of
the mountain meadows.

We traveled to Chamonix, the mountaineering pioneer's birth-
place, where we experienced skydiving and saw jaw-dropping
scenery. Discovering Annecy, dubbed the "Venice of the Alps,"

we strolled along historic canals that murmured history. Not to be overlooked is Grenoble, a thriving city where modernity and tradition coexist amid the foothills of the Pyrenees.

We visited neighboring villages and cities in each chapter, where we were able to take in their distinct attractions. Savoring the culinary delicacies and different cultures of each location, we got a taste of their essence, from the cultural treasures of Geneva to the elegance of Turin.

Beyond the locations, though, we honored the intangible essence of the French Alps, such as the feeling of wonder you get as you climb to the peaks of the mountains, the comfort of a heated hut on a cold night, and the companionship you have with other tourists over a fondue pot.

The memories of the French Alps will cling to you as you go home, calling you to come back. The French Alps will always beckon you back to its embrace, whether it's the appeal of summer's meadows carpeted with wildflowers or the seduction of winter's snow-capped peaks.

So, we say goodbye to the French Alps as the alpenglow covers the horizon in shades of pink and gold. I hope that the moments you've shared and the memories you've collected will always be engraved in your heart. Au revoir and happy voyage, till we cross paths again in this mountain wonderland!

Printed in Great Britain
by Amazon

42763050R00106